More Precious Than Gold

WORDS OF STRENGTH, ENCOURAGEMENT, AND WISDOM

NANCI J. GRAVILL

WESTBOW
PRESS®
A DIVISION OF THOMAS NELSON
& ZONDERVAN

WestBow Press books may be ordered through booksellers or by contacting:

WestBow Press
A Division of Thomas Nelson & Zondervan
1663 Liberty Drive
Bloomington, IN 47403
www.westbowpress.com
844-714-3454

Permission notice: Excerpt from Max Lucado's book *You'll Get Through This* for "Waiting" essay and *Fearless: Imagine Your Life without Fear* for "Walking the Wire" essay.

Back cover:
Photography ~ Cherry Blossom Photography
Hand-blown glass plates (back cover photo) ~ Artist, Shayna Roth Pentecost, https://www.srpglass.net

ISBN: 978-1-6642-5138-0 (sc)
ISBN: 978-1-6642-5139-7 (e)

Library of Congress Control Number: 2021924015

Print information available on the last page.

WestBow Press rev. date: 2/3/2022

This book is dedicated to all the precious people who live in my apartment complex.

We do life together every day. We've shared sad moments, enjoyed laughter and good conversations, given hugs and more hugs, barbecued, spent some holidays together, viewed countless sports games on TV with one another, supported one another through COVID-19, and much more!

Being a part of this season of my life, each resident here holds a special place in my heart. Thank you for being who you are and sharing that with me every day. Through the pages of this book, I pray that every one of you will come to know God in a more personal way.

Inspiration for the book's title:

The law of the LORD is perfect,
refreshing the soul.

The statutes of the LORD are trustworthy,
making wise the simple.

The precepts of the LORD are right,
giving joy to the heart.

The commands of the LORD are radiant,
giving light to the eyes.

The fear of the LORD is pure,
enduring forever.

The decrees of the LORD are firm,
and all of them are righteous.

They are *more precious than gold,*
than much pure gold;
they are sweeter than honey,
than honey from the honeycomb.

They give knowledge to me, your servant;
I am rewarded for obeying them.

None of us can see our own errors;
deliver me, LORD, from hidden faults!

May my words and my thoughts be acceptable to you,
O LORD, my refuge and my redeemer!

—Psalm 19:7–12, 14 (NIV)

Contents

Wisdom for Personal Growth

Self-Reflection

Self-Reflection for You

For Your Spiritual Connections

Reference Section

Acknowledgments

I so appreciated everyone's help in making this project come together. It really took a community of caring people to do so!

Special thanks to John, Ralph, Sue, and Roberta. They were the folks in the focus group study who helped to review the book back when I started writing in 2017. They gave me some great ideas and perspective.

I was grateful Birdie listened to me on many occasions as I sorted out ideas with her. My hat goes off to fellow authors Chuck and Jim for their suggestions of a publisher. Jim Cermak was a great help and has a heart of gold. However, I must say, without Andrew's help, this book would never have been! Andrew, I can't tell you just how grateful I am for your IT efforts, as you helped me out of a really tight spot. I'd still be writing if it weren't for you! The next shout-out is to Don Myers. He helped me in many, many ways. Special thanks to Pastor Rick Duncan from Cuyahoga Valley Church. He recommended some fine books for your spiritual growth. He was so thrilled to be of service, and I loved his enthusiasm and his willingness to be of help.

I just want to mention that several other wonderful folks helped to bring this project to completion. You know who you are, and you all were a blessing. Thank you! Thank you! Branch manager Jason Ensworth at PNC Bank, Parma Branch, was also a great help. Special thanks also to my cousin Bill in Dallas. He gave me advice regarding my photo for the back cover and for marketing the book. And do you know he even posted a new article on my blog from Dallas when I couldn't? Hats off to you, Bill!

Many others prayed for me and encouraged me as I wrote the book. I can only say that "thank you" is not nearly enough for all that each one of you did. Please know that your support and encouragement truly helped to make this book be more precious than gold!

Again, many, many thanks to some really fine folks of God! Your crowns will be waiting for you in heaven!

Introduction

We live in a fallen world. That means that fear, worry, hate, illness, and many other things have become our reality. It all started when a perfect world and our connection to our creator ended. Then, something called sin was introduced. God is perfect, and anything we do that falls short of His perfection is sin.[1] The ideas in this book are designed to challenge your perspectives and provide information to guide you through the personal storms or trials that come to you through this broken, imperfect world in which we live. But more than anything, this book is about recapturing that wonderful connection with God that was lost.

Before our life begins, God places into each one of us unique gifts and talents. God created me with a helper-type personality. I have always recognized people's needs and been concerned about the well-being of others. And as it turned out, nearly all of my work experiences gave me the opportunity to help others too. So, over the years, it's never surprised me to learn from others that one of my spiritual gifts is encouragement. In fact, one of my goals in writing this book is to hopefully encourage you.

Please don't misunderstand me. By writing this book, I'm not saying I have it all together or have all the answers. I don't. But I've learned a lot over the past sixty-plus years though my life experiences, stepping out on faith, taking risks, encouraging myself, counseling and self-examination, earning an education, and God working in my life.

It's true. God wants to do more in your life than just fix your problems. Instead, He wants to change you from the inside out. Right now though, God's trying to get your attention. Many times, He uses our circumstances like our pain, frustrations, disappointments, and other problems to do just that. God used a whole host of things that happened all at once to bring me to my knees. That was eighteen years ago. I went through breast cancer, the death of three family members, the loss of my friends, and the loss of every penny I had invested or saved. Before that time, I knew God was watching over me because I survived three years of substitute teaching, a nearly fatal bicycle accident, four years of therapy on two frozen shoulders, fifteen years of caring for my mother, a lot of counseling, and countless other things. Realizing I had no idea how to manage my life, in 2005 I decided to surrender to Christ, and I let Him direct my steps from that point on. You can find out more about that in the "For Your Spiritual Connections" section in the back of the book, *Learn about a Relationship with God.*

As the world gets darker, I hope these short essays and the "Spiritual Connections" section that follows will help you get ready for heaven. Jesus is coming back. He's coming back soon.

Book Tour

1. *How This Book Can Help You:* Most of all, I hope that this book will help you to remember to take some time each day to let God speak to you (read the Bible)—and you to Him.

2. *How the Book Is Set Up:* It is *a* collection of short essays with a devotional page following each one. I recommend you use a journal of some sort to record your thoughts, prayers, fears, or anything else that's important to you.

3. *Essays*: I've grouped the essays together so they follow the subtitle, "Words of Strength, Encouragement, and Wisdom."

4. *Reflection Concept:* This term means you should talk to God about what you are going through. Ask for His guidance and wisdom to help you make the best decisions and take the best course of action for your life. Also get quiet and tune out other people's expectations and the influence our culture can have upon you.

5. *Pages for Reflection*: Here, take time to think about things or do more reflection and study. Every page also has some directives (directions) to guide.

6. *Bible Verses:* There are many scriptures from the Bible in this book. Take time to meditate on God's Word. It reveals God's power and amazing plans for you!

7. *Versions of the Bible*: Many different versions of the Bible were used in this text, including the Amplified Bible, English Standard Version, and the Message Bible. The

Message Bible is a poetic yet contemporary version of the Bible that may be helpful for understanding a verse.

8. *For Bible Study:* You can always go to biblegateway.com to look at the different versions of the Bible for a scripture.

To Give You Strength

Things Happen for You

Listen to your life. What is it telling you today?

Here's something that you may never have thought of before: things don't happen *to you*—they happen *for you*!

Things happen for you so you'll learn, grow, mature, and become a blessing to someone else. Listen to your life. What is it telling you today? Is it possible that a diagnosis of cancer or the loss of your job can teach you new ways to live? Every experience in life is an opportunity to learn something. Both the pleasant and unpleasant events that come our way have the ability to bring something of great value to us.

Maybe you've realized that gifts or blessings in this life don't always come to you in beautifully wrapped packages. Sometimes blessings come to you when you have an accident, are diagnosed with cancer, learn that your child has autism, or lose someone you love. You may lose a job, but then out of nowhere, the opportunity comes to do something you've always wanted to do. *Things happen for you.* This is why it's important that you pray and exercise your faith, especially when life takes an unexpected turn. Those difficulties you are going through right now are just the things that will allow you to grow and learn more about yourself, others, and God. Those difficulties will change you in some beautiful way so you won't be the same person you were before. Those same difficulties may even bring about an unexpected blessing. But don't be fooled. The way you look at life—your attitude—makes all the difference in how you perceive the things that happen *in* your life.

When stuff happens, there is always the temptation to say, "Hey, look at what terrible thing is happening to me!" You can feel sorry for yourself or realize that God has the situation all taken care of, complete with the answers, before things even materialize.

God has an amazing plan for your life. It's probably just different from the one you imagined for yourself. One thing is for sure: God never promised your life would be easy. What He did promise was to be with you through your difficulties. Remember the difficulties you faced last week or a year ago? Those were part of God's plan to get your attention and to help grow your faith. His plan will also allow you to become a better person. He wants you to have the greatest sense of integrity, the kindest heart, and the best manners, all with an ability to see the best in everyone—exactly the way Jesus did and would today!

Here's God's best plan: Jesus's death and resurrection were the ultimate things that happened for you. They were for your good and the good of everyone.

God is working in your life so that things happen for you!

> And we know that all that happens—happens [for us] for our good if we love God and are fitting into his plans. (Romans 8:28 TLB)

Things Happen for You

Listen carefully. Everything that happens in your life is the result of God's great plan for you. Things don't happen randomly. No. They purposefully unfold exactly in the way God intended them to do so.

And because of His great love for you, God has carefully designed it so that *things happen for you*. Every event during the course of your life is designed to draw you toward God and to His will for your life. Many times, we cannot see the good in our situations until the rain clouds have cleared. Still, no matter what you are experiencing today, trust God to work out the good plans that He has for your life.

Meditate on the scriptures below and record your thoughts. Use your journal to record and explore what in your life has happened *for you*.

- "In the world you have tribulation *and* distress *and* suffering, but be courageous [be confident, be undaunted, be filled with joy]; I have overcome the world" (John 16:33 AMP).

- "'I know the plans I have for you,' declares the Lord, 'plans to prosper you and not to harm you, plans to give you hope and a future'" (Jeremiah 29:11 TLB).

- See also Romans 8:28.

Waiting

Waiting is one of the hardest spiritual disciplines.
Waiting is spelled T-R-U-S-T.
—Dave Samples[2]

Have you heard the remarkable story of Joseph, son of Jacob, that begins in the book of Genesis in the Bible? Joseph learned a thing or two about waiting. He was the youngest brother in the family and his father's favorite. Because of this, his brothers hated him. Scripture says, "Now Joseph had a dream, and when he told it to his brothers they hated him even more" (Genesis 37:5). One day, Jacob sent Joseph out to check on his brothers. They were tending a flock a long way from home. Seeing Joseph from afar, his brothers decided to kill him. But one brother had misgivings. Instead, they sold Joseph to a caravan of traders going to Egypt. In Egypt, Joseph was sold to Potiphar, an officer of Pharaoh and the captain of the guard.

In a strange land away from his family and in prison, Joseph made the best of where he was. And God made sure that he prospered in all he did. In those difficult years, Joseph worked hard, trusted God, and obeyed the authority God placed over him. While many years passed, the years in prison were not a waste. These were the years when God helped Joseph develop such things as trustworthiness, honesty, integrity, courage, honor, and fortitude. Joseph needed those qualities for the future God had planned for him. But it was those in-between times when Joseph waited that a loving God used every situation for Joseph's good. Here's what happened for Joseph and what happens for you, too, as you wait.

From the book *You'll Get Through This* by Max Lucado:

> Joseph emerged from his prison cell bragging on God. Jail time didn't devastate his faith; it deepened it. And you? You aren't in prison, but you

may be infertile or inactive or in limbo or in-between jobs or in search of health, help, a house, or a spouse. Are you in God's waiting room? If so, here's what you need to know:

While you wait, God works. But Jesus replied, "My Father is always working, and so am I." (John 5:17 NLT). Because you're idle, don't assume God is.

While you wait, God works.

Waiting can be tough. So how do you remain patient? When you accept the circumstances of your present situation, that helps you develop patience. And as you do, you'll learn the life lessons that God has for you. Like Joseph, the lessons that come your way now are important for your future. The things that may seem difficult, annoying, or trivial to you now are just the things God will use for your good. And God uses every situation for your good, even if you can't yet see the end result—the blessing He has in mind for you.

But those who wait for the Lord shall renew their strength.
They shall mount up with wings like eagles; they shall run
and not be weary; they shall walk and not faint. (Isaiah 40:31 TLB)

Waiting

This is just an ordinary day, and it seems as if nothing much is going on. But we know that's when God is most at work in our lives. Sometimes it seems like we wait and wait and wait. Although you may feel a little discouraged today, be encouraged, friend. What you're waiting for and need so much will be here soon. God is faithful, and His answers always arrive right on time!

Meditate on the scriptures and quote below. Record anything in your journal that comes to your mind.

- "This is the most precious answer God can give us: wait. It makes us cling to him rather than to an outcome. God knows what I need; I do not. He sees the future; I cannot. His perspective is eternal; mine is not. He will give me what is best for me when it is best for me."[3]

- "[As you wait] … Patience is not the ability to wait but the ability to keep a good attitude while waiting."[4]

- "But those who wait for the Lord [who expect, look for, and hope in Him] will gain new strength *and* renew their power; They will lift up their wings [and rise up close to God] like eagles [rising toward the sun]; They will run and not become weary, They will walk and not grow tired" (Isaiah 40:31 AMP).

- See also Ephesians 1:19–20 (GNT).

Courage

Courage is a state of mind that each of us has
the ability to create for ourselves.

Courage is the best, the highest, and the most commendable response to some real or imagined fear.

Deciding to respond with courage to your situation doesn't mean you're not afraid. And it doesn't mean you won't feel some of the emotions that accompany fear, such as anxiety or some uneasiness. It simply means as you step into the unknown, you're not going to back down from the task at hand, even if any negative emotions do creep up. So you may just decide to "do it afraid," as Bible teacher and speaker Joyce Meyer would say. In the Old Testament, God gave Joshua the job of leading the Israelites into the Promised Land. He told Joshua not to be afraid. What He was really telling Joshua was he would be attacked by many fears, and he'd want to turn back. But he must keep going forward.[5]

Embracing Courage

Faith and trusting God are the best ways to address fear and to help you move forward with courage. But who is your faith in today? Is it in your bank account or people? Or is your faith in the God who created this entire universe and is all-knowing, all-powerful, faithful, and loves you more than you could ever know? To quote a line from a favorite Geico commercial, "That's what it takes, babe!"[6] It takes having faith in a gigantic God to live courageously and drink in victory!

Consider David, the young shepherd boy in the Bible who defeated Goliath with only this slingshot and gobs of faith (see 1 Samuel 17:45). At that time, all the other men lacked courage to face Goliath because each man believed that if he went out against this humungous human, he would be on his own and end up as bird food (1 Samuel 17:44).

But David was different. David's courage came from his confidence in God's promises and God's power to fulfill them. The reality was this: David was not self-confident; he was God-confident.[7]

Ultimately, David's victory over Goliath showed who David depended on and where he placed his faith. Killing the giant without a doubt showed the faithfulness and power of God.[8] Still today, God is well able to slay any giants in your life—smoking, drugs, alcohol, eating disorders, relationship issues, and any other difficulties you are facing. The question is, who is your faith in today?

And let me tell it to you straight. If you are a child of God, the Holy Spirit stands waiting to give you the courage that you need today or at any other time. Therefore, make up your mind not to give in and not to give up.

> Be strong and courageous. Do not fear or be in dread [of them],
> for it is the Lord your God who goes with you.
> He will not leave you or forsake you. (Deuteronomy 31:6 ESV)

Courage

Courage: the ability to keep making forward progress while you still feel afraid.[9]

Sometimes we need to be strong and confident even if we don't feel like we are. Courage is a choice. And fear is the number one way the devil tries to get a foothold into your life, hoping that will stop your ability to move forward and make progress. Instead, God desires for you to put your trust completely in Him. God is with you. Trust Him! Step out! Choose to be courageous! Think about what the little character from *The Hobbit* said:

"Go back?" he thought. "No good at all! Go sideways? Impossible! Go forward? Only thing to do! On we go!" So up he got … And his heart all of a patter and a pitter."

Meditate on the scriptures below. Record your thoughts below if you wish.

- "For God has not given us a spirit of fear, but of power and of love and of a sound mind" (2 Timothy 1:7 NKJ).

- "Have I not commanded you? Be strong, vigorous, and very courageous. Be not afraid, neither be dismayed, for the Lord your God is with you wherever you go" (Joshua 1:9 AMPC).

- "A man of courage is also full of faith" (Marcus Cicero, Roman politician and lawyer, 63 BC).

- See also Deuteronomy 31:6 (ESV) and Psalm 31:24 (KJV).

A New Mental Toughness

It is not the amount of the faith we have—or mental toughness
or resilience—but who is the object of our faith.
—Claire Smith[10]

The truth is many of us know that the strongest people are not those who show strength in front of us but those who win battles we never see them fight.[11]

There are moments when we all need to be strong. Mental toughness or tenacity is any set of positive qualities that helps a person to cope with difficult situations.[12] It's a mental attitude. It's a mindset.[13]

But mental tenacity or toughness isn't just for police officers, sharpshooters in the armed forces, or FBI agents. Life's unexpected moments can cause you to reach for your superhero cape and stand strong when you're a citizen attacked by an intruder in your home, a patient struggling through cancer, an individual navigating a messy divorce, or when you or someone you know is managing any other difficult life situation. Jesus relied on mental toughness for several situations He encountered, especially when He went to the cross.

In Matthew 4:1–11, we see Jesus being tempted by the devil in the wilderness after fasting forty days and forty nights. Weak from lack of nourishment, the devil tried his best but didn't get the best of Him. Why? Jesus exercised mental strength—mental toughness. He never backed down, and He held His ground. What was the key to Jesus's strength? He spoke out God's Word. When the devil fed Jesus a lie, He simply said, "It is written," and quoted the Word of God (Luke 4:1–13). For the Christian, that's where your strength lies as well—speaking out the Word of God. It's filled with power for your life!

Here's the New Mental Toughness

But mental toughness has a deeper and different meaning for the person who has given their heart to Christ. Being mentally tough to a Christian is not about relying on our own strength or kicking our mental toughness into gear. No! It's about kicking our faith into gear. It means to stand and trust fully in Christ.[14] You see, God helps us develop a different type of mental toughness based on reading His Word and standing on His promises. So, as we grow closer to Christ, our reliance on God and His Word helps us move from relying on our own strength to relying on His strength.

But please understand that having faith in the living God never exempts a Christian believer from illness, challenges, obstacles, or even having difficult days to face. But it is those very things that will help each and every believer in Christ persevere as they stand strong through their difficulties. Then they will be able to say:

> He *only* is my rock and my salvation,
> my fortress; *I shall not be shaken.* (Psalm 62: 6 ESV)

A New Mental Toughness

Jesus went to the cross, and it took mental toughness and focus to do so. Gratefully, He was determined to carry out His Father's plan for all of humanity.

Did you realize that when you tap into God's power, you can persevere past any challenges and circumstances—even those that seem impossible? The real question isn't how strong you are but in whom have you placed your faith.

Meditate on these scriptures and quote. Then watch your strong-minded faith kick in!

- "God did not give us the spirit of fear but of power, love, and a sound mind" (2 Timothy 1:7 KJ21).

- If you keep your eyes open,
  If you continue to trust me,
  If you continue to believe,
  If you continue to put one step in front of the other,
  If you continue to live your life as if I'm who I say I am,
  You will catch a glimpse of my glory even in your most difficult times. [15]

- See also Psalm 46:1 and Joshua 1:9 (NLT).

Even in the Storm

One day he got into a boat with his disciples, and he said to them,
"Let us go across to the other side of the lake." So they set out and
as they sailed he fell asleep. And a windstorm came down on the
lake, and they were filling with water and were in danger.
—Luke 8:22–23 (ESV)

All about Storms

We've all seen videos on the news after storms have rolled through places. The photos make us aware of the damage and havoc that occur in people's lives all because of bad weather—all because of storms. Think back to the hurricanes in Houston, the Gulf, Florida, and Puerto Rico in August and September 2017. People's lives were taken, and others lives were very much disrupted by these storms.

Encyclopedia.com tells us a storm is any disturbance in the earth's atmosphere with strong winds accompanied by rain or snow and sometimes thunder and lightning. Storms have a generally positive effect on the environment and on human societies because they are the source of most of the precipitation on which the planet depends.

Personal Storms

So here's the question: if the rain is good for the earth, then what about when the storm clouds form and the rain floods your life? Can your difficulties really be beneficial and have a positive effect on your life? Yes, I believe they can.

First of all, storms get our attention, and in doing so, they help us focus our energies in very specific ways. Secondly, storms have the ability to shape us into the best version of who God wants us to be. That's because storms help us develop strength, compassion, and character. In a storm, you'll find you pray the hardest, study the scriptures more than ever, ask others to keep you lifted in prayer, and even seek wise counsel from a pastor, elder, or well-respected friend. It's a time when you're fully engaged in looking for answers. But more than ever, it's a time when you need to hear from God. No other event besides a crisis can have that kind of effect on your life. So, our storms are not only to stretch us beyond our comfort zone but to draw us closer to God.

Holding Steady in a Storm

Every storm is useful and valuable for your life. The moment you realize this, you'll make every effort to *move with* your circumstances instead of resisting or *moving against* them.

Ideas to Help You Hold Steady in Your Storm

- Keep focused on God. He is your anchor in the storm.

- Label what you're going through an adventure or a journey, not a crisis. Then you'll respond in a much more positive way—instead of producing panic.

- Speak lots of positive words over your life (self-talk) every day.

- Keep a good attitude. This makes things go more quickly and easily.

- Manage your emotions. Every challenge comes with an emotional component to deal with. Fear is a very powerful emotion. Come against it with faith and the belief you *will* make it through.

Here's the Good News

No one goes through life without encountering storms. But the good news is this: rest assured, no storm lasts forever. They always have an end.

> They came to Jesus and woke Him, saying, "Master, Master, we are about
> to die!" Then Jesus woke up and rebuked the wind and
> the raging waves. Suddenly the storm stopped and all was calm.
> (Luke 8:24 NLT)

Even in the Storm

If the storm clouds are forming and the rain is beginning to flood your life, don't worry. Every personal storm is useful and valuable for your life. God is your anchor in the storm. Our storms are there not only to stretch our faith but also to draw us closer to God.

Every day, thank God for the answers He already has for you. God is with you in the storm, and He will bring you safely through it all. And remember, no storm lasts forever! Hallelujah!

Meditate on the scriptures below. Record anything you wish in your journal or below.

- ○ "There is wonderful joy ahead, even though you have to endure many trials for a little while. These trails will show that you faith is genuine … it will bring you much praise and glory and honor on the day when Jesus Christ is revealed to the whole world" (1 Peter 1:6–7 NLT).

- ○ "Count it all joy, my brothers, when you meet trials of various kinds, for you know that the testing of your faith produces steadfastness. And let steadfastness have its full effect, that you may be perfect and complete, lacking in nothing" (James 1: 2–4 ESV).

- ○ See also Luke 8:24[a].

Words Have Power

If you change your words, you'll change your life!
—Joyce Meyer[16]

Here's the bottom line: words have great power! And if you change your words, you'll change your life! Turn to Proverbs 18:21 (ESV) in your Bible. It says, "Death and life are in the power of the tongue, and those who love it will eat its fruits." So that means that the words you choose will either bring you a harvest of good things, or they will bring disappointment and maybe even heartache for your life. You'll reap exactly what you sow.

Words are containers, and they hold emotions, ideas, and thoughts. Bible teacher, author, and speaker Joyce Meyer wrote a book titled *Change Your Words, Change Your Life*. The book's message is that our thoughts and our words are related to the quality of our lives. If we bring together both our thoughts and our words and make then come into agreement with the Word of God, the Bible, we'll see powerful results. And since we all have a circle of influence (friends, family, coworkers), we can speak hope, discouragement, or fear into someone's life. You can complain or be grateful. You can lash out in anger at someone or choose to bless them with words that uplift and encourage them.

Learn to replace the negative things you have been saying with the positive and hopeful words from the Bible. And if you need a good place to start, try my two favorite little words: *I can!* Those words came from a scripture in the New Testament, book of Philippians, verse 13 (ESV), which says, "I can do all things through Him [Christ] who strengths me." Here's another positive example that will make your life better every day. Start saying, "I trust You, God" (see Proverbs 3:5–6).

Also choose words of encouragement and hope. Don't gossip, keep your word, and always tell the truth, just as your mother taught you! And as a result, your life will be better, fuller, brighter, and so far beyond what you could ever have imagined! Here's the best news of all. Words are so powerful that God spoke the world into existence with them! Think about that! And because God is able to do immeasurably more than all we ask or imagine, according to His power that is at work within us (Ephesians 3:20 NIV), replacing your words with His words has the power to transform your life! Philippians 4:13 (ESV) says it best:

I can do all things through Him who strengthens me.

Words Have Power

Life will always have its challenges. But with Jesus in your heart, you're an overcomer. And the way to be even more blessed and be a dynamic champion is to speak out positive words along with the Word of God every day.

Take This Thirty-Day Challenge

Change your words to those that are positive and watch how your life changes. Focus on this bit of truth: you can talk yourself into your dreams or you can talk yourself out of them. It's up to you.

Think about these truths and meditate on the scriptures and statements below:

- "For out of the abundance of the heart the mouth speaks. The good person out of his good treasure brings forth good, and the evil person out of his evil treasure brings forth evil" (Matthew 12:34–35 ESV).

- "A person's words can be a source of wisdom, deep as the ocean, fresh as a flowing stream" (Proverbs 18:4 GNT).

- "Words can poison, words can heal.
  Words start and fight wars, but words make peace.
  Words lead men to the pinnacles of good
  And words can plunge men to the depths of evil."
  (Marguerite Schumann[17])

- See also Proverbs 18:21 (ESV) and Proverbs 23:7 (KJV).

On Your Knees

Fight all your battles on your knees and you will win every time.
—Dr. Charles F. Stanley[18]

One afternoon several years ago, I had a conversation with someone at church. But as I listened to the woman, she told me the strangest thing. She told me to pray.

"Pray!" I said. "What do you mean?" I asked her in a rather worried voice with complete astonishment. I answered, "No! What do I *need* to do?" Again the women told me to pray. You know, I thought she was nuts! And since that time, I've learned that talking to God in prayer and coming to Him as His most beloved child is the best solution to my problems and anyone else's. But here's what we don't always realize as a young Christian: prayer moves God. It summons up all the power in heaven, and it gets God's attention. Prayer is not just talking to God. No. Prayer is the talking part of the most important love relationship you should have in your life. Although He is almighty, all wise, and fully able to work without us, God chooses to work through our prayers. He calls us into a working partnership. Without us, He won't work.[19]

Benefits of Prayer

Have you read the book or seen the movie *90 Minutes in Heaven?* It's the story of Pastor Don Piper, who died for ninety minutes in a car accident in 1989. During those ninety minutes, Don went to heaven as another pastor friend prayed over his dead body. The miraculous events that followed all occurred in Piper's life as a result of prayer. From his book, Piper shared:

I couldn't say it, but I believed then—and still do—that I survived only because a number of people wanted me to. They were relentless, passionate, and desperate, and they believed God would hear them. People prayed for me who had never seriously prayed before. My experience brought people to their knees, and many of them had changed in the process of praying for me to live.

How Do I Pray?

Prayer is something we are told to do because God knows it will benefit our relationship with Him. Make your prayers simple, honest, and from your heart. Also make your prayers based on scripture if possible. That way, you are kindly reminding God of what He has promised in His Word. There is no set time you need to pray. But you may want to get in the habit of being and keeping an attitude of prayer throughout your day. That means pray throughout the day as you feel the need to do so.

Simple Steps to Prayer

- *Praise God.* Praise comes from thinking about His greatness, goodness, and righteousness.

- *Give thanks.* Thank God for all the good things He has done for you.

- *Confess your sins.* Tell God you are sorry for anything you've done. Simply confess and ask for forgiveness. Then ask for the filling of the Holy Spirit.

- *Ask God for your needs.* Philippians 4:19 (ESV) simply tells us God will supply our needs. God cares about His children, so ask Him today.

Note: If you haven't already seen the movie *War Room* released in 2015, do! It teaches the concept of prayer and shows how it works in everyday life. Enjoy the movie!

> Have you ever said, Well, all we can do now is pray?
> "When we come to the end of ourselves, we come to the beginning of God." (Billy Graham[20])

On Your Knees

Jesus went away from the crowds to be alone and pray to His Father. And if Jesus, being God, needed to get away and seek His heavenly Father, why shouldn't we?

God sits in His throne room and sees your prayer request as it comes before Him. But His answers come only when the time is right. However difficult it is to wait for those answers, your prayers are heard by a God who is all powerful and knows what is best for your life.

Now, meditate on the scriptures and quote below. In your journal, record your heartfelt prayers to God. When they are answered, record that too.

- ○ Worry is a conversation you have with yourself about things you cannot change. Prayer is a conversation with God about things He can change![21]

- ○ "Don't worry about anything, but pray about everything. With thankful hearts offer up your prayers and requests to God" (Philippians 4:6 CEV).

- ○ "Let your hope keep you joyful, be patient in your troubles, and pray at all times" (Romans 12:12 GNT).

- ○ See also Luke 6:12 and 1 Thessalonians 5:16–17.

Encouragement for You

Find the Gift

The word *gift*
may remind you of packages wrapped up in
pretty paper and tied with beautiful bows.
Some gifts, however, are of a different kind and
have far greater value for your life.

Life can change in a matter of seconds. And if it does, look for the potential for good the situation is bringing to your doorstep.

First of all, as with any challenge you face, there will be emotional components to deal with—like fear, worry, or uncertainty, for example. Once you get your emotions under control, with your trust fully in God, look for the gift the situation is bringing you. God always provides a gift for us in every situation we are facing, no matter how difficult the situation is.

To find the gift in your particular circumstances, start by asking yourself these questions: "If this situation is in my life, then why is it here? What is it meant to accomplish, or what can I learn from this?" Our present circumstances are really blessings disguised as bad news; they are there to teach us and bless us all at the same time. The challenges you are facing are not here to pay you back for something you did in the past or to make your life more difficult. Instead, think of your present circumstances as God trying to get your attention. Could it be that God thinks you need to adopt some new attitudes so that you can become the very best version of yourself? That's how God works. He's always up to something—something good for your life (Romans 8:28). The trouble is we don't always see it that way! However, it's certainly true that God's gifts to us aren't always wrapped in beautiful, shiny paper and tied up with matching bows. No. Sometimes gifts come to us in the most difficult and unusual ways, and they are not fun at all to unwrap. When

I was nineteen, I went through many months of counseling. It was the most difficult thing I ever experienced. But I stuck with it. Today, the months I spent many years ago telling a counselor about myself keep giving me gifts every day because I am happier and more well-adjusted than I was before. Life got better. Yours will too.

An entry from Sarah Young's devotional book, *Jesus Calling,* tells us how we can realize the gifts that God has for us even in the most difficult situations.

> When you are plagued by a persistent problem—one that goes on and on—view it as a rich opportunity. An ongoing problem is like a tutor who is always by your side. The learning opportunities are limited only by your willingness to be teachable. In faith, thank Me for your problem. Ask Me to open your eyes and your heart through all that I am accomplishing through this difficulty. Once you have become grateful for a problem, it loses its power to drag you down.[22]

Did this week or the other day bring a cascade of difficult circumstances to your door? And are you wondering why things are unfolding in your life in this way? Sometimes God allows things in our lives in order to bring us unexpected blessings. But sometimes those blessings are overlooked. Yet, be encouraged, friend; the difficulties you are facing today will make you stronger and more grateful for your life. Without difficulties, we gain nothing; we are not better people, we are not kinder or more loving, and we are less equipped to navigate life when things happen unexpectedly. The gifts that are of real value for your life don't often come to you in beautiful, brightly colored packages; still, welcome them into your life.

> Look for the blessing in every situation. Things may not be happening the way you planned, but God's plan is far greater. Trust the process.[23]

Find the Gift

Here's the hope-filled message that is meant for you today: there's a blessing in everything—a gift that God sends to you in your situation. This is God's way of helping you to see His hand is in everything that comes your way. He loves you!

Meditate on the definitions and scriptures below. Record your thoughts in your journal if you wish.

- *Gift*: Unmissable opportunity (so good that it should not be missed).[24]

- *Blessing*: A beneficial thing for which one is grateful; an apparent misfortune that eventually has good results (blessing in disguise).[25]

- *Truth:* Sometimes gifts and blessings are not apparent at first. But they are often revealed to us after pain and difficulty.

- "The blessing of the LORD brings [true] riches, And He adds no sorrow to it [for it comes as a blessing from God]" (Proverbs 10:22 AMP).

- "Every good gift and every perfect gift is from above, coming down from the Father of lights with whom there is no variation or shadow due to change" (James 1:17 ESV).

- Other helpful scriptures for study: James 1:2–4; 2 Corinthians 4:8; Romans 5:3–5; Psalm 16:2.

Lifting Others—Lifting Ourselves

Lift ~ Lifting
To raise to a higher position or level.[26]

❖

Encouragement is awesome. It (can) actually change
the course of another person's day, week, or life.
—Chuck Swindoll[27]

The truth is, at some point, every single person will need some encouragement. The word *encourage* comes from the Old French word *encoragier*, meaning "make strong, hearten." But more than anything, encouragement is a powerful tool, and it can be summed it up in one word—giving. It's about giving hope, confidence, courage, and/or comfort to another person.

The Old Testament book of Psalms is one of the best places to find comfort and encouragement in the Bible. Written by many different authors, it shares their prayers and pleas of help, protection, worship, praise, forgiveness, and salvation. The psalmist David wrote many of these 150 psalms while despondent or depressed. Through his writings, he attempted to lift his own spirits and yours as well.[28]

Encouragement is vitally important to our well-being and our success. In fact, encouragement is something God really values. God tells us in the Bible to encourage one another. And it's also the job of the Holy Spirit (third person of the Trinity—Father, Son, Holy Spirit) to encourage us. If you have a relationship with God through Christ, the Holy Spirit is the *Parakletos*; that's the Greek word for "the one who walks alongside us, giving aid, encouraging, building us up, edifying, and comforting us."

Encouragement is also about surrounding yourself with people who are positive and lift you up emotionally. Sometimes, however, we have to encourage ourselves. That's right. Sometimes you'll have to be your own cheerleader, and that means that you say positive things to yourself (positive self-talk) and that you stir up your enthusiasm for the situation you are dealing with. Make up your mind that you'll make it through the things that are before you. If you are struggling today, don't give up. God is still at work in your life even if you can't yet see the outcome your circumstances will eventually produce.

Becoming an Encourager

One thing's for sure, we are not all born encouragers. Encouragement starts with using the most excellent, the most positive, the most complimentary words. First, however, you'll need to realize when someone needs encouragement. That comes through listening to what someone shares or doesn't share about their circumstances. Oddly enough, sometimes the best opportunity to encourage someone comes at the worst time for us. Still, we must learn to respond to others when it's not convenient or easy. Don't let the routine of your day stop you from encouraging someone who needs a special, loving touch. Go the extra mile for Christ.[29]

A word to the wise: put some margin in your life. If your schedule is overloaded, there's no margin—no extra time or room for anything out of the ordinary for an emergency or divine interruption to encourage someone.

Encouragement Ideas to the Rescue!

- *Listen.* This is often the best gift you can give to a person.

- *Offer to help, visit, call, text, or send cards.* Let them know you care.

- *Hugs.* Hugs are the best! They will speak volumes to someone!

- *Prayer.* Ask about their concerns and then pray *with them*.
  And let them know you will continue to pray *for them*.

- *Gifts/goodies.* Bring their favorite goodies or a meaningful gift.

We rise by lifting others. (Unknown)

Lifting Others—Lifting Ourselves

At some point in your life, you'll need some encouragement. Encouraging one another is something God told us to do in His Word. And if God said that, then that's something we all need to do! And if you're not a born encourager, there's no time like the present to learn how to be one! Even when it's not convenient, make the effort to stop and give some encouragement and love. See the interruption as a divine appointment from God, and go do that great *encouragement thing*. I guarantee that you'll be encouraged too!

Meditate on the scriptures below. Then, take a minute to write in your journal several meaningful ways you could encourage someone. What can you say or do?

- ○ "For whatever was written in earlier times was written for our instruction, so that through endurance and the encouragement of the Scriptures we might have hope *and* overflow with confidence in His promises" (Romans 15:4 AMP).

- ○ "Do not use harmful words, but only helpful words, the kind that build up and provide what is needed, so that what you say will do good to those who hear you" (Ephesians 4:29 GNT).

- ○ See also 2 Thessalonians 2:16–17; 1 Thessalonians 5:11; Hebrews 3:13; Romans 15:5.

Fifteen Things to Embrace

Thousands of thoughts come into your mind each day.
Here are some good things for you to reflect on,
embrace, and put in your heart.

1. You and I cannot do life by ourselves; we need each other.
2. Ask for help when you need it!
3. Starting a business, earning a college degree, recovering from surgery, or anything else can be a huge project. But you can do anything one day at a time if you don't give up.
4. Be kind. Everyone is fighting a hard battle.
5. Say yes to new opportunities even if you have to do them afraid.

6. Pray. This unleashes God's power!
7. Laugh often. It will make you healthier and happier.
8. Believe that you can! You have inner resources you've never tapped into that can help you through any storm.
9. Some of God's greatest gifts are the prayers He doesn't answer.
10. Sometimes the best thing you can do for another person is to listen.

11. Whose life have you made better today?
12. Give of yourself, your time, money, and abilities. Give!
13. Smile! Life's more enjoyable that way!
14. Life may be tough, but God is bigger than any obstacle you are facing!
15. Develop a bigger concept of God. He is here to help and guide you. His arms are filled with grace and strength, and He is able to carry your load for you; in fact, He wants to. No matter what you have done or where you have been, God loves you and forgives you!

Fifteen Things to Embrace

Biblical principles and truth will make your life richer, fuller, better. Think of Jesus's promise to you. Jesus said, "I came that they may have and enjoy life, and have it abundantly [to the full, till it overflows]" (John 10:10[b] AMP).

God is bigger and more wonderful than you know. He is there to help you and guide you. He is not the man upstairs! He is all-knowing, full of grace, kind, and loves you more than anyone can and ever will!

Open your heart and meditate on these life principles. Record below anything you feel God is trying to tell you.

- ○ The dark moments of our life will last only so long as is necessary for God to accomplish His purpose in us.[30]

- ○ Trusting God means looking beyond what we can see to what God sees.[31]

- ○ God blesses us so that we might bless others.[32]

- ○ From the list of things to embrace (previous page), what's your favorite thought or inspiration? Meditate and reflect on that.

_____

_____

Embrace this idea:
Begin your day with a conversation with God: pray!

Gratitude

No matter what our circumstances,
we can find a reason to be thankful.
—Dr. David Jeremiah[33]

Growing up, most of us probably heard the phrase "count your blessings." In a nutshell, that's precisely what gratitude is all about. It's about seeing the good in your life and appreciating what you have—and giving thanks to God.

When we are thankful, our focus shifts from our own selfish desires and the pain of our current situations. Expressing thankfulness helps us remember that God is in control and that He sees every need and every heart. Gratitude is a choice that you have the privilege of exercising every day. Think of it as a catalytic converter for your heart: it converts negativity into appreciation.

Gratitude makes us nicer, more trusting, more social, and more appreciative. As a result, it helps us make more friends, deepens our existing relationships, and improves marriages.[34] Being grateful affects our mental and physical health too. Scientific evidence has proven that our thoughts and the emotions they produce have an impact on our well-being. So, friends, open up the channels and let the gratitude flow!

> To the credit of Jesus they were healed [lepers]. Their spines began to straighten, skin began to clear, and smiles began to return. The mass of misery became a leaping, jumping, celebrating chorus of health.
>
> Jesus waited for the ten men to return and say thanks. But only one of them came back. Even Jesus was astonished. Why? Ingratitude.[35]

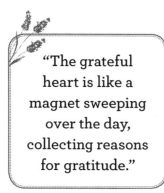

"The grateful heart is like a magnet sweeping over the day, collecting reasons for gratitude."

"A proud man is seldom a grateful man, for he never thinks he gets as much as he deserves." The grateful heart on the other hand, sees each day as a gift. Thankful people focus less on what they lack and more on the privileges they have. "The grateful heart is like a magnet sweeping over the day, collecting reasons for gratitude. zillion diamonds sparkle against the velvet of your sky every night. Thank you, God." [36]

The Bible tells us thankfulness (gratitude) should be a way of life (see 1 Thessalonians 5:18). The truth is the more you compare, the less satisfied you are [with your life.] However, when we are grateful and walking in love, we spend less time looking at what everyone else has and more time noticing what we have been given. The good news is our gratitude places our eyes on God instead of others. [37]

Simple Gratitude Practices

○ *List all your blessings*, great and small!

○ *Bedtime practice*. Print the words *Thankful for Today* on a three-by-five card. Put the number five underneath that. At bedtime, recount five things you are thankful for from that day or things in general. Sweet dreams!

○ *Start a gratitude journal*. Simply list all the blessings from God that you see each and every day.

○ *Look for the gifts in your life*. Talk more about what you like about your life than what you don't like.

Thankfulness is the heart of a person
moving toward God. [38]

Gratitude

Gratitude does something special within us. It overflows into our hearts and changes our focus. It also does so many wonderful things like creates peace, allows us to drop any jealousy or envy, and it fosters the very best thing—humility. Gratitude causes even the darkest places in your heart and your mind to be flooded with light.

> The grateful heart is like a magnet sweeping over the day, collecting reasons for gratitude. A zillion diamonds sparkle against the velvet of your sky every night. Thank you, God. (Max Lucado)

What are you thankful for today?

Meditate on the scriptures and statement below. Then, make a list of your many blessings!

- "In every situation [no matter what the circumstances] be thankful and continually give thanks to God; for this is the will of God for you in Christ Jesus" (1 Thessalonians 5:18 AMP).

- "Lord, with all my heart I thank you. I will sing your praises before the armies of angels. I face your Temple as I worship, giving thanks to you for all your loving-kindness and your faithfulness, for your promises are backed by all the honor of your name. When I pray, you answer me and encourage me by giving me the strength I need" (Psalm 138:1–3 TLB).

- For further study: Philippians 4:6–7; Philippians 4:8; Psalm 9:1.

Wiser—Better

A state of mind that sees God in everything is evidence
of growth in grace and a thankful heart.
—Charles Finney[39]

Think about the various experiences you've had thus far in your lifetime. So often, we tear ourselves down and compare ourselves to others. Sometimes we fixate our minds on where and how we fell short, and sadly, we forget to look at all we've accomplished. So, to lift you up and express the truth of how God sees you today, this message is here to shed light on the different seasons of your life. Of course, the scenarios below may be very different from those you've experienced. Take a deep breath and then take a minute to think about the memorable moments of life that you've enjoyed. God made you a unique individual, and your life has followed its own unique path. Pull back your shoulders and be proud of yourself. You are truly more amazing than you know!

❖

Whether you are thirty, fifty, or a spunky eighty-two years young, through the years you'll probably agree that you have grown mentally, emotionally, and perhaps even spiritually as well. That's because in every season of your life, you've encountered new challenges and learned countless things along your journey. Some would say that it's all about the journey and not the destination. Yes, it's about who you met, what you did, what was said, and the unexpected things that occurred that made your cup full every day. It was the laughter, helping others, the questions and answers, the kids, the grandkids, your neighbors, or your senior friend at church who made you feel needed—that made you feel like your life mattered. Whatever your age, everything you are and whatever you've been through has made you wiser and better in some extraordinarily wonderful ways.

Embracing the daily and weekly challenges that came to your corner of the world I hope has mellowed you into a real pussycat. And the truth is the older you get, I'm thinking the more grateful you are that God has been with you on your journey. If that's not so, that can certainly change today!

Standing up to your challenges and moving forward has matured you, made you stronger, and allowed you to develop a whole lot of resilience. Along the way, you've gained valuable coping skills that taught you to have faith, pray, and seek help if you needed to. Then you raised your kids. What an education that was! And one day out of nowhere, you courageously sat in the passenger seat of your nice new car while your kid drove it around the neighborhood, practicing his driving skills. On other days, you'd shop with your aging parent who got behind the wheel of the motorized grocery store cart. This driving adventure took a lot of courage too! Remember when mom narrowly missed the display of holiday cookies and the two of you broke into infectious laughter? Thankfully, others were laughing too. Mentally and emotionally, today you're wiser and better with a confidence that you didn't have before and a sense of humor you developed even in the most trying of times.

Friends, you are more amazing than you know! Still, sometimes life can feel empty and lonely. But hopefully amid all the chaos and every drop of laughter, you found Jesus and invited Him into your heart. And if you haven't yet heard the good news about the King of Kings, please see the section "For Your Spiritual Connections" in the back of the book and find out why you were created and how much God loves you.

Truth: following Jesus will make you wiser and better!

> Do not turn away from her (Wisdom) and she will guard *and* protect you;
> Love her, and she will watch over you.
> (Proverbs 4:6 AMP).

Wiser—Better

Today, God whispers, "Remember, you are stronger because I brought you through your storms and have shaped your heart through the years. But most certainly you are wiser and better if you know Me [Jesus] and do my work in a world that needs to find hope and a Savior."

Look at your life today. Yes, you've grown and accomplished a lot. Still, give your heart to Jesus if you haven't already. As a loving, gracious God, He wants to give you joy today. Then, on some other lovely day, He'll carry you off to heaven after your purpose here on earth has been completely fulfilled.

Now, meditate on the scriptures below. Record your thoughts in your journal.

- "Do not reprove a scoffer, or he will hate you; reprove a wise man, and he will love you. Give instruction to a wise man, and he will be still wiser; teach a righteous man, and he will increase in learning" (Proverbs 9: 8–9 ESV).

- "Listen to advice and accept instruction, that you may gain wisdom in the future" (Proverbs 19:20 ESV).

- See also Colossians 3:23.

- See the "Spiritual Connections" section to learn more about a relationship with God through Christ.

Wisdom for Your Well-Being

Take a Drink of Great Happiness

Put your ear down close to your soul and listen hard.
—Anne Sexton[40]

Are you wondering about this ancient ritual referred to as providing greater happiness? It's a tradition that's been handed down for many centuries. Many have heard of it but quickly dismiss its value and benefits. It's really quite simple, as this secret of *ancient wisdom* is actually all about a spectacular journey you can take for as long as you'd like. This ancient practice dates back to the fifteenth century.

Which would you choose? Would you rather clean out your closet or take a few moments to reflect and record your thoughts and take a drink of the greatest happiness? I know what most people would say: I'll clean my dirty closet!

Cleaning is a very good thing. It gets rid of unused and worn-out things, makes order where there was none, helps you examine and take stock of things, and provides mental refreshment along with a sense of renewal. It's amazing what a little time and attention will do.

Taking a drink of great happiness provides the very same benefits and more than you get from cleaning your closet. Plus, the great thing is you won't get dirty, tired, or have bags of things to take to Goodwill! Journaling helps you sort the good in your life from the stuff that's no longer helpful, needed, or fitting in your life at the present time. And as you sort through everything, you'll begin to grow and get a sense of order. This will help you go in a direction that is more beneficial and satisfying for your life.

What's All the Fuss about Journaling?

○   Most people are unaware of how journaling can really help them.

- Journaling may take time you don't think you have. And if you don't really understand the benefits, why would you want to invest your precious free time in this way?
- Sometimes we are afraid to face the questions that will provide us with the answers. So it's easier to remain fixed where we are. Quite frankly, we're afraid.
- People think it's about being a good writer and all that stuff like punctuation and good sentence structure. However, journaling is not about how well you write. It's all about you!
- A sense of pride may keep us from the very thing that will in fact help us. In general, journaling may be seen as a self-help tool. And if you have a hard time admitting you need help, this may be a tough thing for you.

One of the Most Important Issues Regarding Journaling

Journaling isn't about your writing skills; in fact, you don't even have to make entries using complete sentences. However, writing is the vehicle you use to express yourself. It's as simple as making a grocery list, a to-do list, or composing a note to a friend. Writing is only the vehicle to get from point A to point B.

Committing your ideas to paper is a mental process. The scary part happens for most of us when we put down our thoughts on paper. We are now giving our concerns a name, and they become real. And some people just don't like to be real; journaling brings us to reality. And yes, sometimes it is easier to deny than have the courage to go the course.

Keeping a Journal

- Date your entries; then you can compare entries and see your progress.
- Write the same time of the day so it becomes a habit.
- Write as much as you want. If you're going through a lot, it's best to journal almost every day. Otherwise, three to five times a week is fine.
- Keep your journal out where you will see it. It will help to establish the habit in your life.
  Thus says the Lord, the God of Israel: Write in a book all the words that I have spoken to you. (Jeremiah 30:2 ESV)

Take a Drink of Great Happiness

Get out some paper and a pen. Write out your thoughts and feelings. Soon you'll be aware of some sweet hidden treasures within your life. As you discover these treasures, your level of contentment and joy will increase. That's what *taking a drink of great happiness* does for you.

Here's an idea: why not take out a journal and write down some notes or any questions you have as you read this book or study the Bible? Invite God to use your journaling experiences to draw you closer to Him.[41]

Meditate on the scriptures below. Record your thoughts using your new and improved skills.

- o "Thus says the Lord, the God of Israel:
  Write in a book all the words that I have spoken to you"
  (Jeremiah 30:2 ESV).

- o "Write the vision; make it plain on tablets,
  so he may run who reads it.
  For still the vision awaits its appointed time;
  it hastens to the end—it will not lie.
  If it seems slow, wait for it; it will surely come;
  it will not delay" (Habakkuk 2:2–3 ESV).

Cleansing Your Soul

Let us cleanse ourselves from everything
that can defile (mar, harm, spoil) our body or spirit.
And let us work toward complete holiness
because we fear (reverence, love) God.
—2 Corinthians 7:1 (NLT)

It's not hard to imagine that some people hang onto things in their homes or their lives because they think it's easier than getting rid of them.[42] In many cases, it may be comforting to hang on to possessions or ways of thinking because they're familiar. But here's the real truth about our baggage: the thing that weighs us down is not our baggage but our decision to carry it.[43] In Matthew 11:28 (NASB), Jesus says, "Come to Me, all who are weary and burdened, and I will give you rest." Jesus offers support and rest, and most importantly, He offers a safe place to rid ourselves of the baggage, the deep concerns, and the hurts from our past that we hold onto in life. The sad thing is, when we carry our baggage, it slows us down, making us less effective for God, and keeps us from leading a truly successful life.[44]

Detoxing Your Soul

Cleansing your soul is not just about the personal extra baggage you carry but about what you consume every day. You may be consuming poison that is hazardous to your soul without even realizing it. And since your soul is made up of your mind, your will, and your emotions, toxic attitudes, behaviors, and cultural influences that you allow into your life put your soul in danger. You can't totally screen yourself from all the toxins in this fallen world, but you don't have to be polluted by them either. Instead, you can choose to detoxify your soul, which is the only way to experience the best life and the abundant life God intended for you to enjoy.[45]

The Detoxing Process

Absolutely everything you allow into your life affects how little or how much you grow spiritually. Everything—from your friends, family, the programs you watch, internet content, and more—affects who you become. More than ever, you don't want to buy into the attitudes and values of our culture—a culture that promotes wealth, independence, and self-centeredness. More importantly, it's a culture that's not God conscious.

Spiritual battles are ultimately either won or lost in the mind. So it's important to pay attention to what you think about. Pastor Craig Groeschel, author of the book *Soul Detox,* advises you to pray regularly for the ability to view the situations you encounter as God sees them. This will allow you to have the right perspective. Every day, ask God to show you which of the thoughts that enter your mind are unholy and displeasing to Him.

Detoxing your soul is also about forgiving others and getting rid of any bitterness and jealousy. These are toxic emotions, and they will prevent you from enjoying your life and truly loving others, which is what Jesus calls us to do. Learn also to express your anger in productive ways without bringing about sin in your response.

Tips to Further Nourish Your Soul

- Do not allow fear to guide your life. Trust God instead.

- Let go of materialism and look to God, not money and possessions, to meet your needs for happiness, significance, and security.

- When you consume media of any kind (television shows, songs, internet articles, Facebook, books etc.), ask yourself these questions: Am I being entertained by sin? Is this pleasing to God? Does this lure me away from Jesus? Then, stop viewing the media that you recognize as toxic.

- Since bad company corrupts good character, set boundaries to protect yourself from being influenced by unhealthy people, and cut off unhealthy relationships with people who are dangerous to your spiritual growth and will not change.[46]

  Let's make our entire lives fit and holy temples for the worship of God. (2 Corinthians 7:1[b] MSG)

Cleansing Your Soul

My friends, God believes it's important that you keep your soul healthy and pure. And as you do, it will lead you ever closer to Him.

Truth: I have learned that we can't effectively fight the Lord's battles in the world while neglecting the ones in our hearts (Christian novelist, Bonnie McKernan[47]).

Thought: Ask the Lord to examine, prove, and try your heart and mind, as if testing a precious metal to determine value and genuineness.

Meditate on these scriptures and the wonderful thought below. Record your thoughts below.

- o "He gave his life to free us from every kind of sin, to cleanse us, and to make us his very own people, totally committed to doing good deeds" (Titus 2:14 NLT).

- o "Turn my eyes from looking at worthless things; and give me life in your ways" (Psalm 119:37 ESV).

- o "Dear friends, let us turn away from everything wrong, whether of body or spirit, and purify ourselves, living in the wholesome fear of God, giving ourselves to him alone" (2 Corinthians 7:1 TLB).

- o For further study: Psalm 26:2; Psalm 119:37; 1 John 1:7; 1 John 1:9.

Renew Your Mind

There is nothing good or bad, but thinking
makes it so.
—William Shakespeare[48]

Proverbs 4:23 (GNT) tells us, "Be careful how you think; your life is shaped by your thoughts." That's because your greatest asset is not your bank account or the property you own. Your greatest and most valuable asset is your mind.

Pastor Rick Warren, author of the book *The Purpose Driven Life,* reminds us that God is far more interested in changing our mind than changing our circumstances.

Pastor Rick Warren, author of the book *The Purpose Driven Life,* reminds us that God is far more interested in changing our mind than changing our circumstances. Yes, you'd like God to take away all of your problems and your pain. But God wants to work on you first, because transformation won't happen in your life until you renew your mind, until your thoughts begin to change. Warren says that one of the most important reasons for "managing your mind," as he calls it, is that your thinking is the key to your peace and happiness.[49]

Renewing Your Mind

Everything you've ever done or will do begins with a thought in your mind. Your mind is so powerful. Here's a revelation: you don't have to think whatever comes into your mind. And did you know that changing the way you think by renewing your mind is a biblical principle that can literally change your life? Is that possible? Yes! It's God working through the Holy Spirit in us that leads to changing the way we think. This happens as we read God's Word and exchange our negative, worldly, and limited mindsets for the positive and generous way God wants us to think. The concept is found in Romans 12:2a (NLT). It tells us:

> Don't copy the behavior and customs of this world, but let God transform you into a new person by changing the way you think.

So, what's the secret to changing your thinking? In 2 Corinthians 10:5 (NLV), it shares the plain truth in this way:

> We break down every thought and proud thing that puts itself up against the wisdom of God. We take hold of every thought and make it obey Christ.

Put simply, we are to get rid of every thought that does not line up with the Word of God and carefully examine what comes out of our mouths and out of our heart sat all times. We use God's Word as the standard because it always gives us the *right* way of thinking—that is, healthy and strong, full of power. Let me tell you a little more about what that means. Adam and Eve were in that lovely garden many years ago, and sin was introduced into the world through them. And sadly to say, sin by its very nature has corrupted our thinking and distorted our minds, especially as humans have moved further away from God. Still, God's Word is truth. It is the very essence of who God is. And the truth contained in His Word is able to transform you. It can change your heart, your mind, and your behavior. But first you must invite Jesus into your heart and begin to follow Him. As you rely on and act on the scriptures with the help of the Holy Spirit, your life will be transformed over time.

Where Science and God Intersect

Practically speaking, Christian neuroscientist Dr. Caroline Leaf says you change your thinking by examining every thought that comes into your mind. If it's not a good or healthy thought, you simply switch to another channel in your brain. In other words, think another thought and replace the toxic thought with a fresh, positive one. This means that, yes, you can control what you think about and create health and well-being for yourself as well.[50] In fact, it's estimated that 75 to 95 percent of our illnesses can be traced back to our thought life.[51] And did you know that the average person has more than thirty thousand thoughts a day? But when we simply think about anything that comes into our head, we help to create the conditions for illness; we, therefore, can make ourselves sick.[52] Research also shows that our emotions like fear, bitterness, jealousy, and hate all trigger physical and chemical responses in the body. It's not hard to feel the poison these negative emotions create.[53] Yet if we choose to forgive others as Jesus taught us or extend kindness or love to someone, those positive emotions will nourish our immune system and trigger healthy chemical reactions in the body.

Practical Ideas—Renewing Your Mind

○ *Right thinking* comes when you always feed your mind something good. Set your mind and keep it set on things above—thoughts of God and what He has done (Colossians 3:2).
○ *Right thinking* is nurtured as you say positive things to yourself (positive self-talk).
○ *Right thinking* comes as you nourish your mind by reading Christian books and the Bible. No Bible? Get one! Buy a version that's easy for you to understand.

Right Thinking = Renewed Mind
Renewed Mind = A Better, Happier, More Peaceful Life

Renew Your Mind

It's a good day to think about how magnificent God is and remember what He has done for you. If some toxic thought happens to creep in, just change the channel and think about the best, the loveliest, the most fantastic things and those things that are just frankly amazing! Most of all, make sure what you are saying lines up with the Word of God. That's *right thinking* and *renewing your mind* in a nutshell!

Meditate on these scriptures. Then record your thoughts below.

- "Finally, brothers, whatever is true, whatever is honorable, whatever is just, whatever is pure, whatever is lovely, whatever is commendable, if there is any excellence, if there is anything worthy of praise, think about these things" (Philippians 4:8 ESV).

- "Do not be conformed to this world, but be transformed by the renewal of your mind" (Romans 12:2 ESV).

- See also 2 Corinthians 10:5; Colossians 3:2; Proverbs 4:23; John 10:10[b] (NLT).

Plant Seeds of Love

When you focus on being a blessing, God makes sure that
you are always blessed in abundance. —Joel Osteen[54]

Farmers plant seeds in the spring and get a harvest later on in the summer or fall. We plant seeds too by what we say and what we do for others. The law of sowing and reaping (Galatians 6:7) is we will reap exactly what we sow. The sad thing is, if you center life around yourself, not only do you miss out on God's best, but you rob other people of the joy and blessings that God wants to give them through you.[55] Planting seeds of love is always about saying or doing good things for others. And when you do, that can grow bountiful blessings (for you as well)![56]

Pastor Brian Houston of Hillsong Ministries in Australia shared this thought: "The purpose of God's blessing is to enable you to be a great channel of blessing to others. If you have nothing, there is nothing you can do for anyone else; if you have a little, you can only help a little; but if you have plenty, there is a whole lot you can do. When you are blessed, you have a mighty foundation from which to impact others. You are blessed to be a blessing."[57]

Blessing others (giving gifts, helping them, or encouraging them with your words) is like getting a double portion. You bless others, and somewhere along the way, you'll be blessed as well. Luke 6:38 (NIV) says, Give, and it will be given to you. A good measure, pressed down, shaken together and running over, will be poured into your lap. For with the measure you use, it will be measured to you.

There are two main reasons why God blesses us. We are blessed first of all just because God loves us. And the second reason is so we can be a blessing to others. When you bless others, you direct God's goodness to them. And as you bless others, you'll find it's the most wonderful thing to know you had a part in making someone's life better.

> You will be enriched in every way to be generous in every way.
> (2 Corinthians 9:11ᵃ ESV)

Plant Seeds of Love

Blessing others may be a new thing for you, and it may take time for you to cultivate this habit. In the beginning, you may have to plant seeds of love on purpose. But the result will be worth it, as the garden of your heart will always be overflowing with blessings from the Lord. Take time today to be good to others, for whoever sows bountifully will also reap bountifully.

Meditate on the scriptures below. How can you bless others? Record whatever you wish in your journal.

- "The point is this: whoever sows sparingly will also reap sparingly, and whoever sows bountifully will also reap bountifully" (2 Corinthians 9:6 ESV).

- "[N]ever return evil for evil or insult for insult [avoid scolding, berating, and any kind of abuse], but on the contrary, give a blessing [pray for one another's well-being, contentment, and protection]; for you have been called for this very purpose, that you might inherit a blessing [from God that brings well-being, happiness, and protection]" (1 Peter 3:9 AMP).

- "Do not let unwholesome [foul, profane, worthless, vulgar] words ever come out of your mouth, but only such speech as is good for building up others, according to the need and the occasion, so that it will be a blessing to those who hear [you speak]" (Ephesians 4:29 AMP).

- See also 2 Corinthians 9:7 and Luke 6:38 (NIV).

Wholeness—Healing

Genuine and lasting wholeness and healing
begin with a relationship wih God.

> What God wants for us
> can be summed up in
> one word: wholeness.

Touré Roberts, founding pastor of the Potter's House in Los Angeles and senior pastor of the Potter's House of Denver, says, "What God wants for us can be summed up in one word: wholeness."[58]

In the grand scheme of things, wholeness means there is no lack in any area of your life—emotionally, financially, mentally, physically, socially, or spiritually. (We'll look at all the different types of wholeness that God desires for you, except financial and social.)

In the Greek language, the word *wholeness* is expressed by one word—*sozo*. It means both salvation or being saved from our sins through Christ and being whole as in set free from illness—to make us whole in every way.

Emotional Wholeness—Hurting People Hurt People

One of the things God's wants for you is emotional wholeness. Have you ever heard the phrase *hurting people hurt people?* Many people who are hurting haven't yet resolved the difficulties that happened years ago in their childhood or in a bad marriage, for example. Even though the past is behind them, those deep wounds don't magically disappear. And at times, an individual may lash out at others as a means of protecting themselves from further hurt and pain. But God wants to heal the hurts of your past. Sometimes that means bringing the pain to the surface again and facing what happened long ago.

Bible teacher and author Joyce Meyer was repeated raped by her father for many years. As an adult, she began to study the Bible. Gradually, God's message of unconditional love began to fill her heart and heal the trauma she had suffered. Over time, God used the pain she had endured since childhood and turned that into something beautiful. God combined her past experiences with her sense of humor and knitted those together with His wisdom into a ministry that reaches out to help people in a variety of ways. For more than forty years now, her ministry has been going strong. Today she helps millions through her books, TV shows (*Enjoying Everyday Life* and *Everyday Answers*), her speaking engagements around the world, and Hand of Hope ministry.

Physical Wholeness—Healing

A lot of us go to doctors and physical therapists to get well. Many times, God uses their skill and expertise to heal us. I have a friend who goes to Hong Kong (China) once a year to see his fiancée and other friends. The practice of medicine there is much different than here in the United States. When dealing with a patient, doctors there ask each one about their lifestyle and diet. Seldom if ever are drugs prescribed. Patients are typically treated with natural remedies like herbs, teas, spices, change of diet, journaling, art therapy, acupuncture, and more. This type of medicine takes account of the whole person—body, mind, and spirit, including all aspects of the person's lifestyle.

Spiritual Wholeness

Wholeness and healing in your life are always about the work of the Holy Spirit—the third part of the Trinity: Father, Son, and Holy Spirit. Once you invite Christ into your heart and begin to live for God and read the Bible, then God begins to change your thoughts, desires, emotions, and attitudes. This transformation in your life can certainly be considered a type of healing. And as you continue to seek God over time, you also will begin to take on the wonderful traits of Jesus: love, joy, peace, patience, kindness, and more. These are called the fruit of the Spirit mentioned below in Galatians 5:22–23[a] (AMP).

> But the fruit of the Spirit [the result of His presence within us] is love [unselfish concern for others], joy, [inner] peace, patience [not the ability

to wait, but how we act while waiting], kindness, goodness, faithfulness, gentleness, self-control.

What Is Spiritual Wholeness?

With emotional wholeness, we realize that God created emotions to express what is happening inside of us. Emotions add zest and richness to our lives. They are actually what makes us human and alive. Spiritual wholeness, on the other side of the coin, is something we all desire. It is the idea that we know there is a deeper meaning to life, and we need to find and understand that for ourselves. It is also so very closely linked to our purpose in life. Without this, we may feel lost and empty inside—like something is missing or just not right. That something that is missing is God. And He purposely created each one of us with a God-shaped vacuum inside of us. Spiritual wholeness has to do with reconnecting with God. When this happens, we can move toward becoming whole and content with our lives. And when you realize how much you are loved by God, well, that will bring all sorts of healing to your life! Then the possibilities are endless for a happy and healthy life!

Friends, lay your burdens at the foot of the cross. Jesus died to take your pain and give you a brand-new lease on life. That's what wholeness is all about. That's what knowing Jesus is all about.

Mental Wholeness—Mental Illness

An estimated fifty-four million Americans suffer from some form of mental disorder in a given year.[59] Mental illness is referred to as *madness* and *insanity* in the Bible. Like other illnesses, such as diabetes or asthma, most with mental illness have periods when they are well and productive, as well as periods when they aren't feeling so well and their overall functioning is low.

While there are degrees of illness (some people are more ill and are more affected by their illness than others), those who suffer from a mental illness are bright, talented, and downright interesting people. They are not their illness. Be kind to your friends or loved ones if they suffer from mental illness. They did not ask for these problems. They want the same things in life that you do: acceptance, love, respect, peace, purpose, and

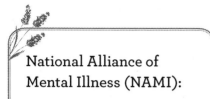

National Alliance of
Mental Illness (NAMI):

Helpline: 1-800-950-6264
In a crisis: Text 741741

relationships, including marriage and children. And like physical healing, God can and does heal mental illness.

Words of warning: Those with mental illness should never stop taking their medication. Stopping medication could cause relapses or serious withdrawal symptoms. Work with your doctor and family, and pray about your condition.

The National Alliance of Mental Illness (NAMI) provides free referral information to doctors and support at 1-800-950-6264. For help in a crisis, immediately text: 741741.[60]

God—Jehovah-Rapha, Your Healer

Many times, God uses a doctor's skill and expertise to heal us when we aren't well. But what if the medical specialists can't help you, or you have some rare disease? Not to worry, friend. God can heal your arthritis or cancer and more. Nothing is too difficult for God! But let's be frank. Healing may take time, and there is a connection between the words that you speak out of your mouth. Are they in agreement with what God's Word says they should be?

In Hebrew, the word *Jehovah* means "God," and *Rapha* means "to heal or to restore." God is Jehovah-Rapha, your healer. Does God heal people today? He most certainly does!

> Jesus continued going around to all the towns and villages, teaching in their synagogues, preaching the good news of the kingdom, and healing every disease and every sickness. (Matthew 9:35 AMP)

Wholeness—Healing

Jesus came that we might have life abundantly. That means plenty, overflowing, more than enough, and above all else that we are whole and healthy people.

If you haven't yet seen the wholeness that God desires for you, if you're a Christian, keep praying and keep standing on God's promises in the Word. Sometimes healing takes time. But by no means is sickness or having problems a way for God to teach you a lesson or punish you for wrong.

Bow your head and say the Lord's Prayer out loud. Especially ask for His will to be done on earth as it is in heaven. There's no sickness in heaven, no lack of anything, no tears.

Meditate on the scriptures below. Record whatever you wish in your journal. God is good. He is able and willing to heal and make you whole in every area of your life!

The Lord's Prayer

Our Father which art in heaven, Hallowed be thy name.
Thy kingdom come, Thy will be done in Earth, as it is in heaven.

Give us this day our daily bread.

And forgive us our debts (trespasses), as we forgive our debtors

And lead us not into temptation, but deliver us from evil: For thine is the kingdom, and the power, and the glory, forever. Amen. (Matthew 6:9–13 KJV)

More scriptures on healing:
Matthew 4:24; 8:13, 16; 9:18, 21–22
Luke 9:42; 17:14–15
Acts 4:9–10
James 5:16

Happy Habits

We become what we repeatedly do.
—Sean Covey[61]

If you've never heard the term *happy habits* before, find a comfortable seat and get ready to hear some interesting ideas that could truly revolutionize your life.

Happy Habit Facts

Your personal habits have a lot to do with your quality of life. Research has found that success or failure in life has much to do with the habits you develop. In other words, the habits you embrace affect your relationships, attitudes, health, and the opportunities that may or may not come your way. The personal habits that you've developed either make your life better or keep you stuck in patterns of behavior that are unhealthy and foster negativity.

Are We Really Happy?

Hopefully, things are going well in your life. But what would happen if you suddenly got diagnosed with cancer, or lost your job, or your spouse wanted to trade you in for a newer model? How happy would you be then?

Most people look to their circumstances to define whether or not they are happy. But the truth is most people just aren't happy. We constantly chase happiness but can't seem to find it.[62]

This whole happiness thing goes back to the Garden of Eden. Adam and Eve did not trust God and disobeyed His instructions. They ate the forbidden fruit. Then they became separated from God and all His ways. They also lost the ability to enjoy all the fruits of the good life that God had created. The lesson is, "In going for what they thought would make them happy, they lost the very things that really do." As a result, humans were separated from God and lost. And the things they tried never brought satisfaction. They were unfulfilled and unhappy.[63] Many of us are stuck there today.

Where Does Happiness Come From?

Your sense of happiness comes from three different components. First, it comes from your own DNA. Second, 40 percent of your happiness comes from the events in your life. Third, long-lasting happiness comes from within and what you value. From your values, you develop habits for work, family, communication, and more. It's your habits that help to determine your overall level of happiness—the level of satisfaction you have with your life.[64]

Developing Happy Habits

Now that you have a better understanding of happiness, what types of habits can you develop that will help you enjoy your life more? What things can you practice daily that will give you the happiness that you want and need? Or, think of it this way: what things will help give you a better outlook on life?

Happy habits involve developing and practicing habits that will help bring you more happiness every day.[65] On the next couple of pages, you'll find some simple things you can do to feel happier—happy habits. Psychologists say it takes from thirty-one to sixty-six days for a habit to be a part of your daily routine. So, don't take on all of these at one time. Maybe choose those that are most important to you and the ones that will be easiest for you to tackle. You don't want to find yourself discouraged, but you do want to be realistic about making changes in your lifestyle. It takes time and effort! You can find almost every one of these happy habits in the Bible. So you know God totally approves of them too!

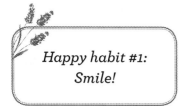

**Happy habit #1:
Smile!**

Happy Habits ~ Simple Ways to Increase Your Happiess

Smiling causes you to appear friendlier, but smiling also has a psychological and emotional effect on you. And for those reasons, smiling makes you feel happier!

People who bounce back more quickly after failure or other difficulties, which we all have at times, enjoy life more.

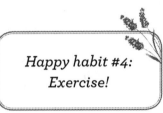

Happy Habit #2:
Be Resilient

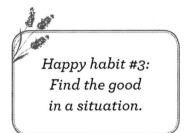

Happy habit #3:
Find the good
in a situation.

There's always something you can learn from a situation. Happiness is a choice.

Did you know that fifteen to twenty minutes, or even thirty minutes, a day of exercise is one of the best things you can do for your bones, your mental and emotional status, your weight, and your overall general health? Exercise will also help you fight against depression, high blood pressure, and dementia. It peaks your happiness meter out at 10. Meaning, on a scale of 1–10, exercise is going to kick in those feel-good chemicals (endorphins). This should be the first happy habit that you begin to incorporate into your life.

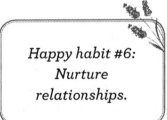

Happy habit #4:
Exercise!

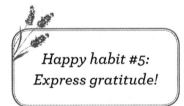

Happy habit #5:
Express gratitude!

Simply saying thank you is a great thing. Gratitude sends a very powerful signal to our brain. Grateful people tend to appreciate the simple pleasures in life. And that helps peak your happiness meter out at a big 10 too! So "Count your blessings, not sheep."

Take time to be with those you love and who are important to you. Even if you have goals and other commitments, don't forget those who are important to you—neighbors, family, and friends!

Happy habit #6:
Nurture
relationships.

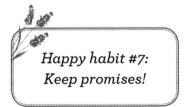

Happy habit #7:
Keep promises!

Do you keep your promises? If you make a promise to someone, no matter how little or big, make sure you keep that promise. People will distrust you if you don't follow through. Integrity is hard to find. But it's a wonderful quality to possess.

Your mom was right. Always be honest, no matter what. In fact, it takes fifteen supporting lies to cover up one lie. Honesty will allow you to lead a much happier and stress-free life.

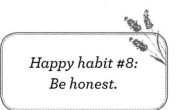

Happy habit #8:
Be honest.

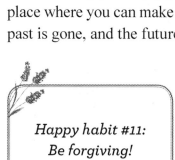

Happy habit #9:
Be spiritually
connected.

Connect daily with your belief in God or some higher power. This will give you strength, especially when you connect with others who believe as you do. Those who study happiness say being spiritually connected is a happiness habit that should be at the core of every person's life.

This may sound really simple, but staying in the here and now will help you enjoy your life more. It is also the only place where you can make lasting changes in your life. The past is gone, and the future has not even begun.

Happy habit #10:
Be present.

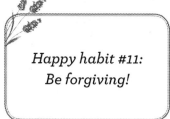

Happy habit #11:
Be forgiving!

Happy people are more forgiving. Everyone in this world makes mistakes, and we ourselves have done so as well. Don't hold grudges. Forgive people and channel that anger into love, which will positively affect all aspects of your life.

Taking life too seriously is never a good recipe for happiness. Being too serious brings on stress, worry, fear, and anxiety. Learn to laugh at yourself and situations, which will in turn produce happiness in your life. Laughter will also help you have a really healthy immune system. Laugh! You'll enjoy much more of your day! "Always laugh when you can. It is cheap medicine" (Lord Byron[66]).

Happy habit #12:
Laugh!

Here Are a Few More Happy Habits You'll Like Too!

One way to rev up your happiness meter is to be engaged in a project or activity that you love and are good at.

Do something you love!

Many folks think this last happy habit (do good) is one of the best happy habits to incorporate in your life. It never gets old, and there is always someone who needs help, love, or encouragement.

Do good!

Give to others, whether it is helping someone, volunteering, or donating items. Giving will always raise your happiness levels. "There is more happiness in giving than receiving" (Acts 20:35 GNT)[67].

Happiness is the spiritual experience of living every minute with love, grace, and gratitude. (Denis Waitley[68])

Happy Habits

God wants us to be the best we can be—healthy, strong, forgiving, grateful, and a person who keeps our promises. These happy habits can help you enjoy your life more every day.

Connect with God in prayer. Next, record any of your thoughts (and/or prayers) in your journal. Last of all, meditate on the scriptures below

- ○ *(Happy habit: Exercise.)* 1 Corinthians 6:19–20

- ○ *(Happy habit: Express gratitude.)* "In every situation [no matter what the circumstances] be thankful *and* continually give thanks *to God*" (1 Thessalonians 5:18 AMP).

- ○ *(Happy habit: Keep promises.)* Proverbs 20:7

- ○ *(Happy habit: Be spiritually connected.)* "Let us hold fast our confession [of faith and cling tenaciously to our absolute trust in Him as Savior]" (Hebrews 4:14 AMP).

- ○ *(Happy habit: Be forgiving.)* Colossians 3:13

- ○ *(Happy habit: Laugh.)* Proverbs 17:22[a]

- ○ *(Happy habit: Do good.)* Acts 20:35 (GNT)

- ○ For further study: Psalm 5:11; John 16:24; Galatians 5:22–23; Proverbs 15:15.

Unspeakable Joy

Think joy, talk joy, practice joy, share joy,
saturate your mind with joy, and you will have
time of your life today and every day all your life.
—Norman Vincent Peale[69]

There's another issue that trumps happiness, and it's one that God has so carefully designed for us. Instead of happiness, God wants us to have something even better. He wants us to have joy. Joy's a bit different from happiness. Pastor Charles Stanley explains it this way: "Joy is a gift from God that enables believers to find hope and peace—even when life seemingly falls apart."[70] Author Kaye Warren defines joy like this: "Joy is the settled assurance that God is in control of all the details of my life, the quiet confidence that ultimately that everything is going to be alright, and the determined choice to praise God in all things."[71]

> "Joy is the settled assurance that God is in control of all the details of my life, the quiet confidence that ultimately everything is going to be alright, and the determined choice to praise God in all things."

How to Cultivate Joy

One way to have joy is to set your mind ahead of time so that no matter what comes up, you'll look for the good in every situation. Also, if you pray about your needs and then cast all your cares on God, as shared in 1 Peter 5:7, you'll soon realize how much more peace you have when you let God take care of things for you. If you start fretting over those issues again, just give them back to God. If God is handling your problems, you don't need to worry.

The Best Advice

Saying good things can also increase your joy. But one thing's for sure: worry will rob you of your happiness (and joy), as it says in Proverbs 12:25[a] (AMP). Anxiety in a man's heart weighs it down. But the good news is this: if you keep your eyes on God and not on your problems, you'll have great joy! The Christian organization Focus on the Family stated, "When good things happen, you may give God credit for it. When bad things happen, you may feel God has turned His back on you.[72] Read Psalms 32 and 51 as David turned toward God amid crises and was rewarded with joy. David wrote these psalms after he committed the sin of adultery with Bathsheba and sins against her husband Uriah. Writing these psalms filled David with peace.[73] But let there be no mistake, joy also comes from knowing God, enjoying what He has done for you, and believing that He constantly cares for you."

Beyond Happiness

Joy is actually the most wonderful gift that God can give us. It's so much better than happiness. Why? Because you can be happy one day but not the next. Instead, joy is a supernatural response to your situation that only God can give you. And you can have joy every day from God. But here's where our discussion of happiness and joy takes yet another turn. This may surprise you, but God's ultimate goal for our lives is not our happiness; it's holiness.[74]

What Is Holiness?

We call a man holy when his heart is conformed in some degree to the image of God and his life is regulated by divine principles. Therefore, holy is used to mean the same as good, pious, godly.[75] Holiness is not about perfection, but it is definitely about moral goodness.

So, you see, our loving, merciful, and full-of-grace heavenly Father ultimately is more concerned about the condition of our hearts than our happiness. Every caring and loving earthly parent wants the best for their children. God is no different. He wants more for His dear children than things that will make us happy for a short period of time. No, God has a much loftier goal. He wants us to grow toward becoming more and more like Him.

> For God has not called us to impurity, but to holiness
> [to be dedicated, and set apart by behavior that pleases Him,
> whether in public or in private]. (1 Thessalonians 4:7 AMP)

Unspeakable Joy

Without a doubt, God would give us the moon if that was the best thing for us. But when it comes to managing the issues of our daily lives, He wants us to drink from a cup that is filled with joy each day. Cultivating joy takes practice. That's because it comes from surrendering our concerns to God as we worship and praise Him even in the midst of our most difficult times.

But here's the good news: believers in Jesus may live lives of extreme joy. Not just being happy, but God says in 1 Peter 1:7–9 (ASV) that you can live a life of unspeakable, inexpressible joy—a joy so incredible we cannot fully describe it. It is not only God's will that we be joyful, but He has made a way for us to find joy through Jesus Christ.[76]

Now, meditate on the scriptures below. Record your thoughts and whatever you feel God is trying to say to you. And if you need to, cast your cares on the Lord. That's real joy!

- "The trying of your faith, being much *more precious than of gold* (which perishes, nevertheless it is tried with fire), might be found unto praise and glory and honor when Jesus, the Christ, is made manifest; whom having not seen, ye [you] love; in whom, though at present [you] see *him* not, yet believing, [you] rejoice with joy unspeakable and full of glory; receiving the end of your faith, *even* the saving health of your souls (receiving as the result [the outcome, the consummation] of your faith, the salvation of your souls)" (1 Peter 1:7–9 JUB/AMP) (vs. 9).

- "All the days of the desponding and afflicted are made evil [by anxious thoughts and forebodings], but he who has a glad [joyful] heart has a continual feast [regardless of circumstances]" (Proverbs 15:15 AMP).

Wisdom for Personal Growth

Get Wisdom

Wisdom is the power to see and the inclination to choose the best and highest goal, together with the surest means of attaining it.
—J. I. Packer[77]

What would you ask God for if you knew He would give you one special thing? Would it be good health, to win the lotto, a better job, a house, or maybe a trip to Paris or Hawaii? One king in the Old Testament asked God for one thing and only one thing—wisdom. King Solomon could have asked for riches, long life, and many other things. Why did he ask for wisdom (see 2 Chronicles 1:11)?

King Solomon was a newly appointed king with a vast kingdom to manage (2 Chronicles 1:8–9), and he wanted to be successful. Therefore, realizing he had an enormous task ahead of him, he needed God's wisdom more than anything else. Solomon also knew that being in a position of leadership (authority) is a trust from God as well as a gift from Him. He was also aware that every leader will stand one day before the King to give an account of this trust, and he didn't want to be ashamed on that day. So he asked for wisdom.[78] One day, you too will give account of the trust and gifts God has given you. Think about what King Solomon was experiencing. He was basically admitting he lacked the knowledge and skill to manage his own situation, but he knew God could help him. What about you? Could it be that you need God's wisdom to manage your life and make the right decisions too?

God's Wisdom Is Supreme

King Solomon was one smart cookie! He valued wisdom because he knew that God's wisdom goes beyond what we as humans could ever know or comprehend. My friend, God's wisdom will always be the highest, the best, the most perfect. It is a supreme judgment overflowing with understanding for your life. As humans, we simply do not possess that kind or degree of insight. His divine wisdom is made available to us in these ways: from the knowledge you gain as you read and understand God's Word and as you seek God in prayer. James 3:17 (GNT) expresses God's wisdom in this way:

> But the wisdom from above is pure first of all; it is also peaceful, gentle, and friendly; it is full of compassion and produces a harvest of good deeds; it is free from prejudice and hypocrisy.

Wisdom Is Your Friend

Certainly we aren't in the position that King Solomon was in. But we all need wisdom every day to manage work, family, our health, and the many decisions we need to make every day. Wisdom is doing right now what you'll be happy with (satisfied with) later on.[79] Looking back, you'll say, "I'm so glad I did that!" Wisdom is an all-powerful spiritual resource that you possess if you have a relationship with God through Christ.

Wisdom is about taking stock of your life and realizing what you need to do and doing it! It's not about sitting on the couch, eating bonbons, doing nothing yet saying, "Oh, that's good advice." Wisdom is your friend. And one day, something will come up, and you'll be glad you were inconvenienced by that medical test or a phone call you didn't want to make.

Wisdom to Discern God's Best

The Old Testament book of Proverbs is an assortment of profound advice that can give you direction for your life. Proverbs 14:12 (ESV) tells us, "There is a way that seems right to a man, but its end is the way to death." The truth this verse is sharing is that God's wisdom helps us discern those things that look really great at first, but then after closer examination, we find it's not right for us at all. Without God's wisdom, we would make painful mistakes and find ourselves in very difficult situations.

Isn't it good to know that God will help you work out the details of your life? But, of course, seeking God's wisdom must be a part of that plan.

> *I*, wisdom, will make the hours of your day more profitable and the years of your life more fruitful. (Proverbs 9:11 TLB)

Get Wisdom

God knows more about you than you know about you. So you see, friend, He's in the very best position to give you all the wisdom you need. Have a decision to make? Need some clarity? Are you at a crossroads? God will gladly give you the wisdom you need. All you have to do is ask.

Now, meditate on the scriptures below. Record your thoughts and whatever you feel God is trying to say to you. Then, through prayer, begin to talk to God about your needs and your deepest concerns. Ask God to give you His wisdom for your circumstances, and He will!

- ○ "If any of you lacks wisdom [to guide him through a decision or circumstance], he is to ask of [our benevolent] God, who gives to everyone generously and without rebuke or blame, and it will be given to him" (James 1:5 AMP).

- ○ "I am Wisdom, I am better than jewels; nothing you want can compare with me. I am Wisdom, and I have insight; I have knowledge and sound judgment … Those who find me find life, and the Lord will be pleased with them" (Proverbs 8:11–12, 35 GNT).

- ○ See also Psalm 111:10, Proverbs 3:5–6, 13 (ESV).

Kindness

Kindness is more than deeds.
It is an attitude, an expression, a look, a touch.
It is anything that lifts another person.
—C. Neil Strait[80]

Kindness is one of those old-fashioned values you don't hear much about today. That's because our culture seems more consumed with making money and getting ahead instead of being concerned about how we treat others. It's too bad that kindness has gotten a raw deal because it's really quite an outstanding quality to have. So here's the scoop on this very precious yet forgotten commodity. Kindness is all about being friendly, generous, and considerate. It's also about affection, warmth, gentleness, concern, and care. Kindness is a form of love and compassion. As a Christian, it's one of the fruits of the spirit and evidence that the Holy Spirit is working within you. Kindness can be a powerful tool to combat the sting of self-centeredness and apathy in our culture.

Jesus set the example for us. Much of His life was about doing kind deeds. He had active compassion for others. That means He not only noticed the needs of people, but He helped others in the midst of their difficulties. What can we learn from Jesus? If we step back two thousand years ago, here's what we would have seen—one kind act, Luke 5:12–13 (NIV):

> While Jesus was in one of the towns, a man came along who was covered with leprosy. When he saw Jesus, he fell with his face to the ground and begged him, "Lord, if you are willing, you can make me clean."
> Jesus reached out his hand and touched the man. "I am willing," he said. "Be clean!" And immediately the leprosy left him.

Caused by flesh-eating bacteria, leprosy has been around for thousands of years. Still, it's a cruel illness, and those affected have to isolate themselves from others because it's highly contagious.[81] But in the scripture above, out of the kindness of Jesus's heart, in one swoop He healed the man from his social isolation, his physical pain, and the destruction of his entire physical body. His healing was experienced immediately, scripture says. Imagine the joy that this man experienced! His whole life was changed! Praise God!

Kindness Today

Jesus's healing of the leper as well as many other healings was an act of kindness and compassion. Jesus showed us that kindness matters. He also showed us it takes a compassionate heart to cause an individual to reach out and give comfort, love, help, or encouragement to someone else.

As mentioned earlier, kindness isn't something that's really talked about much in our culture, probably because it's not thought of as being very important. Yet, thankfully, one man did think it was important: Tim Tebow. He is a former NFL quarterback who tried to make his return to the NFL with the Jacksonville Jaguars. With the help of Tim's foundation, seven years ago here in the States and in Europe "Night to Shine" was created. It's a prom for special needs individuals that takes place right around Valentine's Day. To date, 655 churches sponsor this special event. An extra bit of kindness is offered, as their caregivers and families are also pampered while their loved one is having the time of their life.

The efforts of many help make this night a memorable one. Every Night to Shine is really a great party blessed by the kindness of Jesus working through others.

> The man who tries to be good, loving, and kind finds life, righteousness, and honor. (Proverbs 21:21 TLB)

Kindness

Kindness is a very powerful thing. But with our heads buried in our cell phones, are we missing the opportunity to be kind to others when they need it?

Jesus was kind. That tells me that God the Father must be kind too. Sometimes people speak about God as if He were an old ogre waiting to dump misery into their lap. Oh that's ridiculous! That's just not true! He loves you. After all, He sent Jesus to die for you and then gave you the Holy Spirit to help you live your life!

Meditate on all the scriptures here. In your journal, write about this marvelous thing the world needs more of—kindness. How can you show kindness to others?

- "Be kind to one another, tenderhearted, forgiving one another, as God in Christ forgave you" (Ephesians 4:32 ESV).

- "As a Father is kind to his children, so the Lord is kind to those who honor Him" (Psalm 103:13 GNT).

- "But the Spirit produces love, joy, peace, patience, kindness, goodness, faithfulness, humility, and self-control. There is no law against such things as these" (Galatians 5:22 (GNT) (the "Fruit of the Spirit").

- For further study: John 8:3–7; Luke 5:17–20, 24[b]–26 (NIV).

Do the Happy Dance

Consider how your attitude contributes to someone else's day. The truth is that your attitude directly affects whether or not you are a blessing or a curse.
—Pastor Charles Swindoll[82]

Did Jesus ever dance? We don't know for sure. Many think He probably danced at the wedding in Cana, where He performed His first miracle and turned water into wine. Yet the kind of dancing we're talking about here has to do with your attitudes, not about you gliding gracefully on the dance floor. But certainly you can always crank up the music and dance in the morning. That's a great way to start off your day. And how *do* you start your day? Frankly, you can get up and be depressed and crabby, or you can get up and choose to be happy. Doing the happy dance is all about enjoying every moment, being good to others, and seeing that the glass is half-full. Grumpy? You can always flip the switch to happy and choose to have a good attitude, even in the midst of your most difficult times. It's really up to you.

What about Jesus? What attitudes did Jesus have and leave for us to follow?

Jesus's Attitude

For three short years, Jesus walked the earth healing and teaching. One thing you can say about Him, Jesus was always approachable. Being approachable is a really important thing. Why? People don't come to you with their concerns and wanting to be healed if you have a crabby, negative, "don't bother me" attitude. No. Jesus was never like that! He knew people needed kindness and love. And on top of everything, Jesus was humble. He was also patient and treated women as first-class citizens in a day when that wasn't so.

What Does Jesus Expect from Us?

When you become a follower of Christ, you have a new heart, a new mind, and a new life in Christ. All that said, what type of attitudes does God expect you to have in this new life of yours? Jesus expects you to follow His example. Jesus had a special kind of patience and compassion. He took time to look around and care about others. Jesus had a unique ability in that He slowed down enough to notice, but he certainly didn't sit around. He was out walking. He was moving in the towns and in the countryside. And in the middle of his activity, he noticed people.[83]

Jesus demonstrated an active compassion for others. Active compassion means actually getting involved in someone's problem by helping them to find a solution. Read the story of the Good Samaritan in Luke 10:25–37. This good fellow helped the traveler who was beaten and robbed traveling on this way from Jerusalem to Jericho. Everyone else could have cared less, for they avoided the traveler in need of help, including a priest. But as Christians, we are to have the compassionate attitude that the Good Samaritan had. That means we are not to turn a blind eye to the problems we see in our world. No! We are to get out there and help when people are left homeless, unemployed, or abused. We are to help the victims of sex trafficking and help the widow and the orphans and more. That's what active compassion is all about—lending a hand to others in need and seeing them through until they can get on their feet again.[84]

But let's be realistic. Hurry is a part of our culture. So allow some extra time in your schedule so you can slow down enough to notice others and help with their needs. That's exactly what Jesus did.[85]

> May the God who gives endurance and encouragement give you the same attitude of mind toward each other that Christ Jesus had.
> (Romans 15:5 NIV)

Do the Happy Dance

Jesus gave love and kindness to others, and He shared the truth with those who wanted to hear it. Before you go out the door each day, put a smile on your face and one in your heart! Those are the best things you could ever wear. Attitude is everything! And that's precisely why you need to hang out with God today and every day and practice your happy dance moves!

Meditate on the scriptures and quote below regarding "attitudes of Christ." What attitudes did Jesus exhibit and set as examples for us? Record any thoughts if you wish.

- ○ "Walk *continually* in love [that is, value one another—practice *empathy and compassion*, unselfishly seeking the best for others], just as Christ also loved you and gave Himself up for us" (Ephesians 5:2 AMP).

- ○ "We cannot change our past. We cannot change the fact that people act in a certain way. We cannot change the inevitable. The only thing we can do is play on the one string we have, and that is our attitude" (Chuck Swindoll[86]).

- ○ "Are we called to be like Noah? Yes. Are we called to be like the Good Samaritan? Yes. But not simply because they are positive examples to inspire us to righteousness. These stories point us to Christ" (Jen Wilkin[87]).

- ○ See also Matthew 6:33, 9:27, 14:14; Luke 10:36–37; Philippians 2:3; Philippians 2:5.

Walking the Wire

The only known antidote to fear is faith.
—Pastor Woodrow Kroll[88]

Most of us will never walk a tightrope, but we face things that scare us every day.[89] For some, fear is about taking an elevator, and for others, it may be flying in an airplane. At one time or another, fear has gripped each one of us and caused us to shrink back from doing the very things that we should.

Nik Wallenda was born into a family of aerial artists, a seventh-generation member of the amazing Wallenda family. From a young age, Nik wanted to walk the tightrope—and he did. For years, he trained and worked together with his family. Then, in 2017, a tragic family accident brought fear to Nik's doorstep for the first time and forever changed his life. And when you do your job as Nik does, forty, sixty, one hundred, or more feet above the ground, walking a tightrope above Niagara Falls, the Grand Canyon, Times Square, and the active Masaya Volcano in Nicaragua, you can't afford to let fear take a hold of you. Over time, God helped Nik conquer his fears. He wrote about the experience in his book *Facing Fear*.[90] What about you? Is some fear holding you back today?

Fear: The Whole Truth ~ Nothing but the Truth

The truth is fear is a very real thing, and it's not from God. Fear is a learned response. It can also be a result of your imagination or lack of information. Yet the presence of fear in our lives can cause us to shrink back so much so that we may not accomplish the purpose(s) that God has for our lives. Bible teacher and author Joyce Meyer believes that fear is a tool the devil uses to try to destroy our lives. However, if you are a follower of Christ, God promises to be with you wherever you go. Therefore, we can quiet our fears, fulfill our callings, and be strong and courageous with the help of God's spirit that works within us.

How can we fight fear?

Weapons to Fight Fear

Did you know there are 366 scriptures in the Bible that address the issue of fear? God knows us so well. He gave us one scripture for each day to mediate on, plus one more for leap year. On the other side of the coin, there are 366 scriptures in the Bible on faith. That makes a total of 732 scriptures to encourage us and lift us up above our fears. But it's not enough just to know there are scriptures that can lift you out of fear. You actually need to know what those scriptures say. Ephesians 6:16–18 (ESV) are referred to as the "Sword of the Word." It's one of the weapons in the toolbox that you can use to overcome the antics of the evil one. You may not realize it, but there's a spiritual war going on. You are breathing oxygen right now that's in the air, yet you can't see it—but it's there! The same is true of evil or the devil. Even though you can't see it, it's still there.

To fight in this war, this spiritual battle, take your own fear-filled words and replace them with God's Word. For example, if you say, "I can't do that. I'm afraid," use the scripture found in 2 Timothy 1:7 (NKJ), which says, "For God has not given us a spirit of fear, but of power and of love and of a sound mind." Meditate on that scripture. Say it over and over again. Get it deep down in your spirit. When you start believing His Word, you'll break free from your fear.

More Faith ~ Less Fear

Each sunrise seems to bring fresh reasons for fear. They're talking layoffs at work, slowdowns in the economy, flare-ups in the Middle East, turnovers at headquarters, downturns in the housing market, upswings in global warming. The plague of our day, terrorism, begins with the word *terror*. Fear, it seems, has taken up a hundred-year lease on the building next door and set up shop. Oversized and rude, fear herds us into a prison and slams the doors. Wouldn't it be great to walk out?

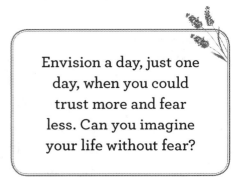

Envision a day, just one day, when you could trust more and fear less. Can you imagine your life without fear?

Imagine your life, wholly untouched by angst. What if faith, not fear, was your default reaction to threats? If you could hover a fear magnet over your heart and extract every last of dread, insecurity, and doubt, what would remain? Envision a day, just one day, when you could trust more and fear less. Can you imagine your life without fear?[91]

For some of us, going to the dentist produces great fear, while for others, spiders are the enemy. Because God knew how we were wired, He gave us a huge arsenal of weapons, composed of 732 scriptures from His Word. These scriptures dispel fear and encourage us to put on faith. It's simple. Put His Word into your heart and mind. But there is a kind of fear that is good and healthy for you. It's the fear of the Lord. It's all about respect and reverence for God. This type of fear helps us run to God, instead of running away from Him.[92]

Think about these truths from God's Word. Say them over and over until you really believe them! Use your journal to express your thoughts about untold fears you may have.

- "For God hath not given us the spirit of fear, but of power and of love and of a sound mind" (Timothy 1:7 KJ21).

- "I sought the LORD [on the authority of His word], and He answered me, And delivered me from all my fears" (Psalm 34:4 AMP).

- "The Lord is the strength of my life. Of whom shall I be afraid?" (Psalm 27:1 KJV).

- See also Psalm 34:4 (MSG); Matthew 6:30–33; Matthew 10:31; Romans 8:31; and 1 John 4:18 (ESV).

You Gotta Grow

You've got to continue to grow, or you're just like
last night's cornbread—dry and stale.[93]

Nola Ochs from Jetmore, Kansas, graduated from Fort Hays State University (FHSU) in Fort Hays, Kansas, in 2007 at the young age of ninety-eight! As of May 14, 2007, she officially became a Guinness World Record holder for being the oldest person in the world to become a college graduate.[94]

After taking a little time off to help with the family's wheat harvest, Mrs. Ochs started working on her master's degree. As of her hundredth birthday, she was also a teaching assistant at the university. Nola kept learning and growing right up until her death at age 105 in December 2016.[95]

Intellectual Growth—Lifelong Learning

Throughout your life, your goal should be to keep growing, maturing, and becoming a more vibrant person. And in doing so, lifelong learning should be something you practice. Why? Because sitting home without learning anything new can be deadly. Here's what you should know: learning new things creates new pathways in the brain. This is important so that you don't develop dementia. Dr. Daniel Amen is a psychiatrist and a brain disorder specialist. He shared this: "Like a muscle—the more you use your brain, the stronger it gets." On the other hand, when you stop learning, your brain starts dying.[96]

Spiritual Growth

If you are a believer in Christ, then you realize that everything in your life is connected to your relationship with God. Think of a good friend you love and want to spend time with. A relationship with God works exactly the same way. The time you spend with God builds your relationship with Him. God is your dear friend, and the more you get to know Him, the more you will trust Him and appreciate His work in your life. Learning more about God will bring changes to your goals, values, character, attitudes, relationships, and how you use your finances. Like intellectual growth, spiritual growth also has benefits for your life. Growing spiritually will increase your enthusiasm for what God is able to do and what He is doing currently in your life. Spiritual growth also brings those wonderful qualities of Jesus, known as the fruit of the Spirit—love, joy, peace, patience, and so on. And, friend, the more you know the Father and have seen His loving hand in your life, the more peace and contentment you'll have with your life.

There are several things you can do to learn more about God and His will for your life. Below are several examples of things you can do intentionally to help you know God better.

Spiritual Growth Plan

Set reasonable spiritual goals for the year. Ideas include the following:

- Read the entire Bible in a year—or two.
- Join a Bible study or prayer group.
- Read several Christian books.
- Memorize scripture.

Helpful Books to Read

- *Battlefield of the Mind* by Joyce Meyer
- *Knowing God* by J. I. Packer
- *The Reason for God* by Tim Keller
- *Spiritual Disciplines of the Christian Life* by Donald Whitney
- *Secrets of the Vine* by Bruce Wilkinson
- *Morning and Evening a 365 Day Devotional* by Charles Spurgeon
- *Choosing Forgiveness* by Nancy Leigh Demoss

Let me repeat what I've said before. The more you know the Father and have seen

His loving hand in your life, the more peace and contentment you'll have with your life. That's what spiritual growth is all about!

Growth: Wrapping It All Up!

It may seem as if you aren't growing at all—because up close it's hard to tell that you're making progress. Growth is different for all of us. But here's a great takeaway: it's a wonderful thing if you only compare yourself to yourself and say, "I'm better than I was yesterday!"[97]

I'm not who I want to be, but thank God I'm not who I used to be.

You Gotta Grow

Are there things you'd like to explore and do? Everyone has some sweet, secret longing. Would you like to learn how to tap dance or do the tango? Perhaps you'd like to visit distance lands like Nepal or Tanzania. Growing is about learning, stepping out, and becoming more of who God made you to be. Trying new things is great. But it's equally important to keep growing spiritually. This will allow you to know God better and love Him more.

Take a minute to relax. Then thank God for His many blessings or the events of today. Or in your best voice, you may want to sing praises to God on high.

Meditate on the verses below and record below anything that comes to your mind.

- ○ "You therefore, beloved, knowing this beforehand, take care that you are not carried away with the error of lawless people and lose your own stability. But grow in the grace and knowledge of our Lord and Savior Jesus Christ. To him be the glory both now and to the day of eternity. Amen" (2 Peter 3:17–18 ESV).

- ○ "So don't lose a minute in building on what you've been given, complementing your basic faith with good character, spiritual understanding, alert discipline, passionate patience, reverent wonder, warm friendliness, and generous love, each dimension fitting into and developing the others. With these qualities active and growing in your lives, no grass will grow under your feet … no day will pass without its reward as you mature in your experience of our Master Jesus" (2 Peter 1:5–8 MSG).

- ○ See also 2 Peter 1:5–8 (explore several different Bible versions).

The Green Bean Club

All about Love ~ 365 Days a Year!

The Green Bean Club is about any day, any weekend, or any holiday for that matter.[98]

Once upon a time, there was this fun-loving family in Seattle, Washington. They had three adorable young girls. And they were very fortunate because they had a good, caring mom. And when you're a good mom, it's important to you that your kids eat their vegetables. So the girl's mom would say, "It's the Green Bean Club!" And all they had to do to join the club was eat their green beans. And of course, they always ate them because the Green Bean Club sounded really fun, and no one wanted to be left out.

The Green Bean Club's Secret and Success!

The real secret to the club's success was that the girls' mom was very clever. She took ordinary green beans and made them seem really cool. But for our purposes, this club is really about something much bigger than eating your green beans. It's about the fact that we all want to be a part of something; we all want to belong. Being part of a family usually fulfills that need. Families make us who we are as they nurture, encourage, and teach us. They also help mold our personality and character. Besides all that, a family is the place where we experience holiday traditions with food, decorations, music, and perhaps funny Aunt Izzie. She always bakes ten pies, brings her cute little Schnauzer, and drives a cute VW bug convertible.

But not everyone has a family or place to go to connect with others who love, value, and accept them. Many people spend holidays alone. That's sad. So, the Green Bean Club is a way of making new friends and making someone else's life better—just like God told us to do.

OK, so what should you make of this green bean situation along with silly Aunt Izzy? How does this apply to you?

The Green Bean Club Takeaway

See if anyone you know will be alone this holiday. If it's not a holiday, invite them over for meatloaf on Tuesday. It only takes a minute to reach out and care. Now we're not only talking Green Bean Club, we're talking God's Green Bean Club! Philippians 2:4 (AMP) says it best:

> Do not *merely* look out for your own personal interests, but also for the interests of others.

The Green Bean Club

Here's the question: do you hear God's voice or feel a nudge in your heart today? Perhaps God is asking you to sprinkle some of His love here and there. You'll have fun, make some new friends, and feel full of smiles deep down in your heart for doing good for someone else. OK! Now we're talking God's Green Bean Club!

Open your heart and meditate on the scriptures below. Record below anything you feel the Holy Spirit is telling you.

- ○ "If someone says he has faith but he has no works? Can that faith save him? If a brother or sister is without clothing and in need of daily food, and one of you says to them, 'Go in peace, be warmed and be filled,' and yet you do not give them what is necessary for *their* body, what use is that? Even so faith, if it has no works, is dead, being by itself" (James 2:14–17 NAS).

- ○ "Do not *merely* look out for your own personal interests, but also for the interests of others" (Philippians 2:4 NAS).

God-Given Purpose

At birth each of us was endowed with a unique gift, something
we were born to do or become that no one else can achieve the
way we can. God's purpose is that we bear abundant fruit and
release the blessings of our gift and potential to the world.
—Dr. Myles Munroe[99]

Disclaimer/note: I know you will enjoy this true story about Candy Christmas. Candy
had a medical issue and did what was best for her. Please consult your medical team
and family for the best course of action to treat any medical condition that you are
experiencing. And of course, season it all with prayer. Thank you!

❖

God gives each one of us a reason for our existence; He gives us a desire to find
meaning and purpose for our lives. He didn't create us to be sitting around bored and
unproductive. The interesting part of this is God does not tell us how to express that
purpose. You are free to be a doctor, teacher, writer, produce manager, or whatever it is
that interests you. However, the ultimate goal is that you use your life to bring glory to
God by being the best at what you do.

Meet Candy Christmas

A talented singer with the voice of an angel, Candy Christmas (that's her real name) sang
gospel music from the age of thirteen with her family's group, the Hemphills. She also
won six Dove Awards and another for singing with the group Heirloom. In 1984, she
was also nominated for Contemporary Album of the Year for her solo recording *Heart
Afire*. Candy grew up in a Christian home, and her father was a minister. She knew the

scriptures well and believed in a sovereign and loving God who had a good plan for her life. [100]

Around 2005, at the height of Candy's career, she left the road as a recording artist. At that time, her life was at an all-time low. Severely depressed to the point where her doctor recommended she be hospitalized, the singer took another approach to her depression. As Candy recalls, she literally gave her way out of her depression by investing in the lives of the homeless who lived under the Jefferson Street Bridge in Nashville, Tennessee. It all started with a big pot of jambalaya that she made and a desire to get beyond her pain. With that, she began to feed the poor and the homeless.

"Some nights we'll have 500 people under that bridge. [101] In the summer we have nearly 1,000 people coming to the bridge," she said. Since homelessness has hit an all-time high in Nashville, the Bridge Ministry is a vital part of helping to address this problem. [102]

"We feed the attendees at the beginning of the service," Ms. Christmas commented. "Then we invite them to stay for church under the bridge. At the end of the evening, we give away new or like new clothing, toiletries, groceries, and a bicycle. Those who stay until after church are loaded up with all sorts of things. It fills our hearts. There is no joy like walking away from the bridge and seeing these people with so much stuff they can hardly carry it. They often bring their friends with them the next week." [103]

"I was born into a record deal," Candy said. "It's just what I did. If I didn't join in, I would be home and the bus rolled on without me. However, what I do now with the Bridge Ministry is because I have a purpose." [104] "The Jefferson Bridge folks don't need a hand out, she said. They need a hand up. If they didn't have our help they'd be digging in a dumpster for food each night."

Over time, as she poured her life into the Jefferson Bridge street people, Candy found her own life and the debilitating pain of depression lifted. God helped Candy find her real purpose, and she realized at the same time that these words of Jesus were so true:

> It is more blessed to give than to receive.
> (Acts 20:35 TLB)

God-Given Purpose

This basic question confronts each one of us: Why am I here? What is the reason for my existence? What is the purpose of my life? Here's the answer: "Man's chief end is to glorify God, and to enjoy Him forever."[105]

What are you passionate about today? Take out your journal and let those answers just flow out onto the page. Ask God for His help today, especially if you are searching for your purpose. But as always, a life full of meaning and purpose starts with Jesus.

- ○ "For I know the plans I have for you—declares the LORD—plans for your well-being, not for disaster, to give you a future and a hope" (Jeremiah 29:11 CSB).

- ○ "But those who wait for the LORD [who expect, look for, and hope in Him] Will gain new strength *and* renew their power [and purpose]; They will lift up their wings [and rise up close to God] like eagles [rising toward the sun]; They will run and not become weary, They will walk and not grow tired" (Isaiah 40:31 AMP).

- ○ See also Psalm 32:8.

Choose to Forgive

Forgiveness is for you—not the other person.
… [It] releases you from your past
and frees you to live life fully.
—Barbara J Hunt[106]

No one is perfect. We all make mistakes. And no matter how hard you try, realize that there isn't a single person dead or alive who hasn't done or said something to displease or hurt another. Sometimes the hurtful words are intentional, and other times they're not. That means that every person at some point in their life will have to think about saying, "I'm sorry," or "Please forgive me," for something.

Choose Forgiveness

Forgiveness is a choice. It takes a lot of energy to hold on to a grudge. It's far better to let it go and channel that energy into love and then give that love away to others. But on the other side of the coin, forgiveness is a very healthy thing to do. While melting away bitterness, anger, and shame, it releases positive thoughts, feelings, and feel-good chemicals in the body. When everything is all said and done, forgiveness works to restore relationships, making the bonds between everyone stronger.

When you choose forgiveness, it produces a stronger immune system and your body works harder to fight illness. Observing this strong connection between forgiveness and illness, two doctors at the Cancer Treatment Centers of America introduced a new technique to their patients called "forgiveness therapy." They noticed that when someone chooses forgiveness, it produces the most miraculous outcome, alleviating many undesirable effects of disease.[107]

The Other Side of Forgiveness

You probably think of forgiveness as forgiving some other person. But sometimes we must extend forgiveness to ourselves. In fact, that may be the hardest person for you to forgive.

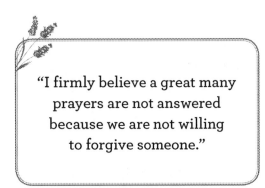

"I firmly believe a great many prayers are not answered because we are not willing to forgive someone."

Dwight L. Moody, founder of the Moody Bible Institute, said, "I firmly believe a great many prayers are not answered because we are not willing to forgive someone."[108] Moody's comment refers to Mark 11:25, which states, "Whenever you stand praying, if you have anything against anyone, forgive him [drop the issue, let it go], so that your Father who is in heaven will also forgive you your transgressions *and* wrongdoings [against Him and others]."

Forgiveness—At the Cross and Beyond

Forgiveness is *the* fundamental concept upon which Christianity revolves. God stands ready to forgive us, and He sent His son to do so by dying on the cross for all of humanity. Weak and near death, on the cross, Jesus said, "Father, forgive them; for they do not know what they are doing" (see Luke 23:34).

Ruth Graham, daughter of the late Reverend Billy Graham, said the first step toward forgiveness is to ask the Holy Spirit to work in you. Next, ask the Lord to make you willing to forgive.[109] Pat Robertson, host of the Christian talk show *The 700 Club*, answered a viewer's question: "How do I get forgiveness from my head to my heart?" Pat gave a great answer. He said, "Stop focusing on the negative and start asking God to bless that individual."[110]

What's the Takeaway?

Forgiveness is something God commanded us to do—and we must! Otherwise, if we don't forgive someone, how will God forgive us (see Mark 11:25)?

> He that cannot forgive others breaks the bridge over which he must pass himself; for every man has need to be forgiven. (Thomas Fuller[111])

Choose to Forgive

It's really tough to measure all the good things forgiveness produces, like good health or freedom from guilt and shame. Forgiving someone may be the hardest thing you'll ever have to do. But it's worth it.

Here's your challenge: Get busy and pray for the person(s) who have hurt you. Ask God to bless them. And slowly your heart will turn, and the forgiveness song will keep playing over and over again in your heart. It's a really lovely melody when you hear it.

Think about these truths from God's Word (or quotes). Repeat them until you really believe them! Use your journal to express your thoughts about anyone you need to forgive, including yourself.

- ○ "Be kind to one another, tenderhearted, forgiving one another, as God in Christ forgave you" (Ephesians 4:32 ESV).

- ○ "Happy is the man who learns to forgive" (unknown).

- ○ "Forgiveness is for you - not the other person. … [It] releases you from your past and frees you to live life fully" (Barbara J. Hunt).

- ○ "And when you stand and pray, forgive anything you may have against anyone, so that your Father in heaven will forgive the wrongs you have done" (Mark 11:25 GNT).

- ○ For further study: Matthew 18: 32–33, Mark 11:25, Luke 23:34.

An Anchor of Hope

Hope
is the thing with feathers
that perches in the soul
and sings the tune without the words
and never stops at all.
—Emily Dickinson, American poet (1830–1886)[112]

About Hope

The dictionary defines the word *hope* as "to wait for eagerly." Yet, regardless of that definition, in our culture today, hope means something completely different. Today it means something that may or may not happen. Yet, looking at the languages of the Bible, the Hebrew and the Greek, together they tell us hope means we should be looking for and anticipating something good to happen. Why? It's all because of God's faithful and loving nature.

What Is Hope?

Hope is something that is priceless. That means hope is not something I can give you, and you can't get it at a department store or pick it up at a drive-through window. You must develop this positive belief for yourself.

Where Is Your Hope?

The company Philosophy, now owned by Coty, Inc., developed a unique skin care line. All their products have been created around the concept of *hope*. Their moisturizer bottle reads, "*Hope in a Jar* ~ where there is hope there can be faith ~ where there is faith miracles can occur." What's your hope in a jar or the hope that you hold on to?

Here's a true story about hope.

Holding onto Hope

Dutch Holocaust survivor Corrie ten Boom (1892–1983) knew very well how important it was to have hope. During World War II, Corrie's family hid refugees in their home through the Dutch underground. At some point, an informant turned the family in, and the entire family was sent to a Nazi concentration camp. After their parents' death, Corrie and her sister Betsie were transferred to several more prison camps. But it was their faith and hope in Jesus that helped them survive the harsh conditions with little food, lack of heat, no air-conditioning, strip-search showers, and crowded quarters that brought lice. They also endured the cruelty of the Nazis prison guards while living with uncertainty alongside other prisoners. [113]

An Anchor of Hope

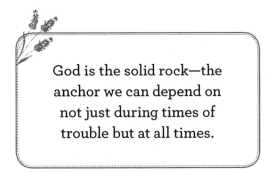

God is the solid rock—the anchor we can depend on not just during times of trouble but at all times.

If you've ever owned a boat or navigated a ship, then you know that an anchor has an important job. It provides stability and safety, which keeps the ship secure in both calm and treacherous waters. [114] This is exactly what God does when His children put their hope in Him. Therefore, He is our stability, our anchor when life events rock our world. But more than that, God is the solid rock—the anchor we can depend on not just during times of trouble but at all times.

Why God Is Your Anchor of Hope

Just like each and every individual, God has a set of personal characteristics that never change. God is always faithful, nonjudgmental, and loving, and He always keeps His word. By His very nature, God is your healer, your provider, your protector, your peace, your good shepherd, your creator, your father. That's just who God is. He's not like anyone you know. That's because He is perfect, without flaw—righteous. So when life's difficulties come our way, and they will, our rock—our anchor and our hope—is Christ.

He will keep you safe and protected until the storms clear and the sky is blue again. That's His promise to His children.

Hope is called the anchor of the soul (see Hebrews 6:19) because it gives stability to the Christian life. But hope is not simply a wish (I wish that such-and-such would take place); rather, it is that which latches on to the certainty of the promises of the future that God has made.[115]

If you fear, put all your trust in God: that anchor holds.[116]

When the world says, "Give up,"
Hope whispers, "Try it one more time." (author unknown)

An Anchor of Hope

Hope is the happy anticipation that something good is going to happen. And it will! But the bigger issue is where or in whom are you placing your hope? Where is your anchor set (your security or firm foundation) in difficult times and other times as well?

Think about these hopeful thoughts:

- Hope, too, is the sweet song in your heart when there is no reason for one! Having hope will give you courage (see Job 11:18). Whatever your circumstances are today, stay hopeful that God has the answers for you—because He does![117]

- A little hope in your heart will always lift you up and keep you positive. Hope replaces those scary feelings deep inside with this thought: *It's possible!* Hope whispers to you, "The best is yet to come!" You can never go wrong when you choose to have hope, when you put your hope in Christ!

Meditate on the scriptures below. Record (in your journal) whatever comes to your mind.

- "We put our hope in the Lord. He is our help and our shield" (Psalm 33:20 NLT).

- "Then you would trust [with confidence], because there is hope; You would look around you and rest securely" (Job 11:18 AMP).

- See also Hebrews 6:19.

Perfect Love

Love is patient and kind; love does not envy or boast; it is not
arrogant or rude. It does not insist on its own way. Love bears all
things, believes all things, hopes all things, endures all things.
—1 Corinthians 13:4–7 (ESV)

From the very first moment you came into this world, you needed love in order to thrive as much as you needed air to breathe. Love is essential for healthy development and a well-adjusted life. Jesus showed us over and over that love is the most powerful and satisfying way to live your life.

Loving Correctly

A family friend died about nine years ago. His son said a few words about him at the memorial service. He said his father taught him how to love correctly. In other words, his father set a good example for his four children about what love is and what that looks like played out in everyday life.

Love is all about action. It's full of hugs, telephone calls, cooking, giving, guiding, complimenting, listening, encouraging, or being there just because. What about you? Are you putting your love into action? Are you loving correctly?

A New Love Phenomenon

Things can go haywire without love. But what if we learn how to give love in the right way? There are an endless number of languages and dialects spoken around the world. Still, there's yet another language that everyone speaks and will respond to no matter where you were raised or what language you learned growing up. This language is referred to as your love language. It's very simple: we all give and receive love differently. When we understand these differences, we can communicate love so much better to one another. So practicing the love language phenomenon can transform your relationships and your life.

Psychologist Dr. Gary Chapman studied and introduced this revolutionary idea about love.[118] He shared this: "It became apparent to me that what makes one person feel loved isn't always the same for their spouse or partner." As a result, Dr. Chapman made an interesting revelation. He observed five distinctive love languages, and he's written about them. You can learn more at Dr. Chapman's website: 5lovelanguages.com.

Types of Love Found in the Bible

Throughout the Bible, you will read about God's great love for you. If we look at the Greek language, we'll learn a lot more about what God has to say about love. That's because the Greek language is more sophisticated and provides greater detail than English. There are eight different types of love found in the Greek language, and four of them are mentioned in the Bible.

The first type of love found in the Bible is eros love. It's a romantic kind of love. Then there's storge love, which describes the bond that develops between parents and children, and brothers and sisters.[119] The third type of love is called philia love. This Greek term describes the powerful emotional bond seen in deep friendships. This is how the city of Philadelphia, City of Brotherly Love, got its name.[120]

God's Perfect Love—Agape Love

Love is something we all want and look for—for our lives. But sadly, we look to the wrong things to satisfy us—money, career, education, adventure, fame. The plain truth is these things don't bring us peace or happiness. And all of them are dead ends in themselves. There's only one lasting type of love that can nurture us and make us whole—*God's love*.

God's love is called agape love. It is the most perfect and wonderful of all the types of love found in the Bible. It's God's unconditional love that He has for you and for me. It's a divine love that is perfect, unconditional, sacrificial, and pure. It is the highest form of love you'll ever experience. It's the also the highest form of love that exits.

God loved us so fully, correctly, completely, and perfectly that He sent us a Savior. Jesus understood what it was like to be human. He rested. He ate. He cried. He loved us deeply. Why else would He take on the sins of the world and go to the cross for all of humankind?

It has been said that God loved us so perfectly and correctly that the shape of true love isn't a diamond—it's a cross. [121]

It has been said that God loved us so perfectly and correctly that the shape of true love isn't a diamond—it's a cross.

(For more on God's love, see the information on a *Relationship with God* located in the section titled "For Your Spiritual Connections.")

Perfect Love

Every person has a God-shaped vacuum inside them. Only God can fill that place in your heart with His agape love—a love that is perfect, unconditional, sacrificial, and pure. It is the highest form of love that exists. Perfect love is not a diamond ring from Jared's. No. Perfect love is Jesus, who died on the cross to set you free from sin in order to bring you back into a relationship with God. Truly, that is perfect love indeed.

Challenge: This week, think of someone that could use a blessing—and be one! That's God's love in action.

Meditate on the scriptures below. Use your journal to express what you've experienced regarding God's love.

- "Since you are God's dear children, you must try to be like him. Your life must be controlled by love, just as Christ loved us and gave his life for us" (Ephesians 5:1–2 GNT).

- "Do everything in love" (1 Corinthians 16:14 NIV).

- "I pray that you may have your roots and foundation in love, so that you, together with all God's people, may have the power to understand how broad and long, how high and deep, is Christ's love" (Ephesians 3:17b–19 GNT).

- See also John 13:34–35; Romans 8:35, 37; 1 Corinthians 13:4 (NIV); Galatians 5:22; Ephesians 5:1–2; Colossians 3:13b–14 (GNT); Hebrews 10:24.

New Beginnings

There are better things ahead than any we leave behind.
—C. S. Lewis[122]

New beginnings can bring a fresh start to your life. Change is never easy. But in the long run, it is oh so worth the risks and the opportunity to follow what God has put in your heart.

Every ending is the start of a new beginning. Whether you're facing an ending, a new beginning, or both, trust God and look for the greater purpose these new opportunities are bringing you.[123] One thing is for sure: God's plan is bigger and better than what you would have planned for yourself. I know it doesn't always look or feel like that, especially at first. Yet, what if we went back and asked the twelve disciples and the apostle Paul about that? I am sure they would agree that God is a Father who always knows best. Today, you might also ask if God's plan is bigger and better of Bible teacher and author Joyce Meyer, who was repeatedly abused by her father for years, and atheist-turned-Christian Lee Strobel. He is the former award-winning legal editor of the *Chicago Tribune* and best-selling author of more than twenty books. They too would tell you without a doubt that God specializes in giving people a fresh start.

What about These New Beginnings?

Twelve ordinary men had no idea of the new beginnings that were up ahead for each of them. From the start, Jesus made it clear to twelve fishermen that He would make them into something different. "Come, follow me, and I will make you fishers of men" (Matthew 4:19 EHV). That's exactly what He did. He taught the disciples to share with others, connect people to God, and minister to those who were in need.

Each day must have been a true adventure with Jesus. Scripture tells us Jesus healed the sick, cast out demons, raised people from the dead, performed other miracles, ministered to the crowds that gathered, and much more. The disciples must have wanted to pinch themselves. Were these new beginnings with the Son of God for real?

God Brings Your New Beginnings

But let's be honest. It's God who brings the new beginnings to your life. Have you gotten a new job, made a new friend, or found that a new situation came knocking at your door? God is always at work in your life whether you realize it or not. So, every difficulty, every heartache, every problem can be an opportunity for a new beginning. They are all opportunities to see God work in your life or someone else's. Proverbs 16:9 (AMP) shares this truth:

> A man's mind plans his way [as he journeys through life], But the LORD directs his steps *and* establishes them.

New Beginnings—The Meanest Man in Texas

This true story shows the power of God working in one man's life. Read how Clyde Thompson was forever changed.

When Clyde was a teenager, he skipped church with his family and went hunting. One Sunday afternoon in 1929, at seventeen years old, he got into a scuffle with some men and killed them. Feeling great remorse, he took full responsibility for the murders. He then became the youngest man on death row at Huntsville Penitentiary.

The prison chaplain called Thompson "the man without a soul." Still, trouble continued to follow him, and he got into a fight and killed two other prisoners, now making it a total of four people he had killed. In solitary confinement, out of boredom, he asked for a Bible. He thought he'd prove the Bible wasn't from God but was full of contradictions. But the more he studied, the more he became convinced it was God's truth. And he came to realize that Christianity was man's only hope. Clyde Thompson began to change. Even the guards noticed it. Later, he was released and returned to death row. Because he made such an impression on the prison administration, they finally released him and let him return to life on the outside.

Continuing to study his Bible, he took a two-year Bible course from a college in Tennessee. Other doors opened for him, and he became a husband, father, a minister, and later a chaplain for the Lubbock County Jail. Eventually, after more than twenty-eight years in prison, the state of Texas gave him lifetime parole.

Clyde Thompson will go down in God's record book as one of the greatest soul winners his generation would ever know. Clyde Thompson, the meanest man in the state of Texas, literally led hundreds of men, women, boys, and girls out of the streets of alcoholism, out of the streets of drugs, and to the foot of the cross of Jesus Christ. Clyde Thompson, the meanest man in the state of Texas, was transformed when he allowed the Word of God and the love of God to take hold of his life.[124]

> The God who made us also can remake us.
> —Woodrow Kroll [125]

New Beginnings

It's God who brings the new beginnings to your life. God is always at work in your life whether you realize it or not. If you're a follower of Jesus, you know firsthand about the new beginnings in your life. Some folks' stories are more dramatic than others, as they'll tell you about how they were delivered from drugs, alcohol, crime, or cancer. Your story is unique—just like you!

In the sweetness of the moment, pray and ask God for His wisdom today for your life. Ask Him to guide you and make the path ahead smooth that leads to your new beginnings.

Meditate on the scriptures and thoughts below. Record (in your journal) whatever comes to your mind.

- When you invite Jesus into your heart and become a follower of Christ, God sets up some new beginnings for you. "When someone becomes a Christian, he becomes a brand new person inside. He is not the same anymore. A new life has begun!" (2 Corinthians 5:17 TLB). Please also see the "Spiritual Connections" section for more on a new life in Christ.

- "Brethren, I do not regard myself as having laid hold of it yet; but one thing I do: forgetting what lies behind and reaching forward to what lies ahead, I press on toward the goal for the prize of the upward call of God in Christ Jesus" (Philippians 3:13–14 NAS).

- See also Isaiah 43:19 and Lamentations 3:22–23 (MSG).

Self-Reflection

Self-Reflection

God will meet you where you are in order to take you where He wants you to go.
—Tony Evans[126]

A doctor was interviewed one night on television. He talked about changes in our culture that have had an impact on every one of us. Compared to thirty or forty years ago, we are now more concerned about self than others, we're more interested in finding ways to get rich and live the so-called good life, and there's been an increase in the desire for independence. Gone too are the close-knit communities where we enjoyed a sense of friendship and family. The doctor cited these changes in our culture as the reasons why more people have depression and go for counseling. Gone is the time when we used to reflect on our lives. Reflection used to take place when a friend or loved one listened to us as we sat and talked with them about some of our thoughts, dreams, and situations where we needed to make decisions. The word *reflect* grabbed my attention. What I heard that night inspired me to write this book.

What Is Self-Reflection?

Self-reflection is a process that helps you sort out issues in your life by talking to a friend or family member. And as they listen, many times the answers you need become clear. Today, however, most reflection is accomplished through counseling or psychotherapy.

Self-reflection involves looking at yourself, including the life path you're on, your values, how you treat others, your goals, and your dreams. And certainly it's about God's plan for your life. As I said earlier, it's a process that involves getting quiet and tuning out the noise of life, meaning other people's expectations for you and the influence our culture can have upon you as well. These two things can affect your thinking and the choices you make.

How Self-Reflection Works

Turn off the television, cell phone, and computer and set aside time to get quiet and listen to what God has to say about your life. There's no set schedule or particular way to do self-reflection. Read, pray, sing, praise, and/or just sit quietly. But don't be surprised if it takes more than a day to hear God's loving thoughts and desires for your life.

Self-Reflection Exercises

On the next several pages, you'll find some exercises to help you with spiritual self-reflection. These exercises are optional. However, folks discover the most glorious things about God and themselves. So you might not want to skip them!

Self-Reflection for You

God knows how to bring us healing and how to walk us out of our pain from our past experiences.

Take a Little Time to Reflect
Beauty for Ashes

Beauty for ashes is a promise found in Isaiah 61:1–3[a] in the Old Testament of the Bible. The message of this scripture is simply God knows how to bring us healing and how to walk us out of our pain from past experiences. All He asks is that you leave your past pain, hurts, and disappointments behind you and keep them there. Then, God promises to give you beauty for those ashes—the things you've left behind with Him. Now God is able to transform you so that you are truly beautiful—more beautiful inside and outside than you've ever been before. Please read the scripture below.

> The Spirit of the Lord God is upon me, because the Lord has anointed me to bring good news to the suffering and afflicted. He has sent me to comfort the brokenhearted, to announce liberty to captives, and to open the eyes of the blind. He has sent me to tell those who mourn that the time of God's favor to them has come, and the day of his wrath to their enemies. To all who mourn in Israel he will give: beauty for ashes; joy instead of mourning; praise instead of heaviness. For God has planted them like strong and graceful oaks for his own glory. (Isaiah 61:1–3[a] TLB)

What ashes from your past can you let go of today? Write down the specific things you want God to help you let go of—pain, hurts, loss, disappointments. Share it all with God. If you keep those things behind you in the past, the result will be that you will be more beautiful and alive than you've ever been before. That's a promise from God to you.

God cares about you.

That's especially why you need to leave your problems with Him.

Take a Little Time to Reflect
At the Feet of Jesus—Casting Your Cares

God cares about you. So don't be worried or anxious. He's got your back. And because He cares about you, He wants you to be free to enjoy your life. That's why you need to leave your problems with God. This is called casting your cares, and the concept can be found in the New Testament in 1 Peter 5:7.

God also tells us to leave our worries (anxieties) with Him, as He wants to carry them for us. Then, go about enjoying your life! God will have the best answers for you at just the right time! Please read the scriptures below.

> Casting all your cares [all your anxieties, all your worries, and all your concerns, once and for all] on Him, for He cares about you [with deepest affection, and watches over you very carefully]. (1 Peter 5:7 AMP)

> Do not be anxious *or* worried about anything, but in everything [every circumstance and situation] by prayer and petition with thanksgiving, continue to make your [specific] requests known to God. (Philippians 4:6 AMP)

The connection between these two scriptures is a simple and powerful one. As you trust that God cares about your anxieties and everything else about you, express them to God in prayer. Prayer is trust turned toward God.

Make sure you read those two scriptures carefully and wholeheartedly, realizing God is giving you wonderful advice that you should follow every day of your life!

Leave all your worries with Him, because He cares for you. Isn't that a great idea? What concerns will you give to Jesus today? Write them below. Remember He cares about you, so let go of those worries and commit them to prayer.

Miracles are things that can't be explained by natural or scientific laws. They are the work of God.

Take a Little Time to Reflect
Miracles—Water into Wine

What Are Miracles?

Miracles are things that can't be explained by natural or scientific laws and are considered to be the work of God. Think of when Jesus turned the water into wine at the wedding at Cana. That was a miracle and the first one that Jesus performed in His ministry. Find John 2:1–5, 7–11 in your Bible and read the scriptures.

> This, the first of His signs (attesting miracles), Jesus did in Cana of Galilee, and revealed His glory [displaying His deity and His great power openly], and His disciples believed [confidently] in Him [as the Messiah— they adhered to, trusted in, and relied on Him]. (Verse 11)

Miracles of Healing

If you prayed to be well and it happened over time, God healed you. But miracles of healing are a bit different. A miraculous healing is something that happens in an instant. An example of this is when Jesus healed the paralyzed man in Mark 2:10–12 (AMP). Please read the account below.

> "But so that you may know that the Son of Man has the authority *and* power on earth to forgive sins"—He said to the paralyzed man, "I say to you, get up, pick up your mat and go home." And he got up and immediately picked up the mat and went out before them all, so that they all were astonished and they glorified *and* praised God, saying, "We have never seen anything like this!"

Now, What about Your Miracles?

What miracles of healing or otherwise have you seen in your life? Write down any wonderful works of God that you can remember.

What do you believe about God today?

God can do everything you believe.

Take a Little Time to Reflect
God Can Do Everything You Believe

This part of the journey is all about what you're thinking. That is, what is God really capable of doing in your life and in others' lives? Then, on a much larger scale, what is He able to do for our world? Take some time to reflect on the two issues below. Record anything here that is tugging at your heart. Beforehand, however, take time to read in your Bible the account of the Centurion soldier and his strong belief in the power of God, found in Matthew 8:7–10, 13 (AMP). A portion of the scripture is below.

> Jesus said to him, "I will come and heal him." But the centurion replied to Him, "Lord, I am not worthy to have You come under my roof, but only say the word, and my servant will be healed.

○ We all are at different places in our spiritual journey. So, what is it you believe about God today? What do you believe He is capable of doing in your life right now?

○ God is there to help and guide you. His arms are filled with grace and strength, and He is able to carry your load for you. In fact, He wants to. No matter what you have done or where you have been, God loves you and forgives you!

Keeping the above statements in mind, do you have any ideas about how you can develop a bigger concept of God—one that's larger and more glorious than the one you already have? In other words, how can you begin to trust Him more?

Prayer is powerful.

Have you experienced its amazing effects in your life?

Take a Little Time to Reflect
Prayers and Praise

Prayer is just simply talking to God about what's on your heart. Did you realize that the early Christians experienced supernatural events through prayer? For example, there was a time in the Bible when King Herod began to persecute members of the church. At this particular time, the disciple Peter was arrested and put in jail. The church prayed for Peter's release. And he was released!

Here's little bit of what happened (verses 7–8). Still, you'll want to read the entire account in Acts 12.

Suddenly an angel of the Lord stood there, and a light shone in the cell. The angel shook Peter by the shoulder, woke him up, and said, "Hurry! Get up!" At once the chains fell off Peter's hands.

- ○ Read Acts 12:4–17 and learn about the miraculous things that occurred as a result of prayer.

- ○ Think of several times when prayer brought the miraculous to your life.

Record these events below. What did you learn about God and about prayer?

- ○ Take a few minutes to write out your prayer list. Be sure to include your family, friends, our country, folks who need healing, people you want to share Jesus with, and our world that needs peace and Jesus! Don't forget your own needs too.

Set aside a time each day to pray for these important items on your list.

For Your Spiritual Connections

Spiritual Connections
Your Soul's Destination—Will It Be Heaven?

I've had some very honest conversations with people over the past year. And through those conversations, I found a reoccurring theme when it comes to leaving this physical world and becoming a citizen of heaven at the end of this life. Most people really believe they are going to heaven after they die. I asked a few people quite frankly, "How do you know you're going to heaven after this life?" Each person's response was the same. "Because I'm a good person," they said. That may be true on some level, yet how good do you have to be to be as good as God? You see, nobody could ever be as righteous, holy, perfect, or free from sin as God is.

Friend, the truth is you don't go to heaven because of all the good deeds you've done over your lifetime. God has another plan, a much better plan, and it's not based on your works. Yet God makes salvation and heaven available to everyone who accepts His free gift—to those who accept His Son. Going to heaven after this life has nothing to do with what you've done (it's purely grace) but everything to do with what Jesus has done.

Here's What Really Happens

At the appointed time when you have completed your purpose here on earth, your physical body will die. When this happens, your soul will either go to heaven or to hell for all of eternity. As I said earlier, most people think it's all the good works that they have done throughout their lifetime that determines where their soul ends up. That's not true! The Bible tells us in Matthew 7:13–14 (ESV), "Enter by the narrow gate. For the gate is wide and the way is easy that leads to destruction, and those who enter by it are many. For the gate is narrow and the way is hard that leads to life, and those who find it are few." I know you must be thinking, *What does that mean?*

Jesus tells us in John 14:6 (AMP), "I am the [only] Way [to God] and the [real] Truth and the [real] Life; no one comes to the Father but through Me."

The Bible makes it clear there is no other way to heaven and to have eternal life than through Jesus. Jesus is the narrow gate that is mentioned above. No other person or religious figure except Jesus ever died in all of history for forgiveness of our sins. Think about that! That's what makes Christianity different from any other religion—Jesus's death on the cross and His resurrection. And, friends, Jesus's triumph over death showed us not only His power (God's supernatural power), but that same power is still alive today and living in the hearts of many followers of Christ through the third man of the Trinity: the Holy Spirit. Beyond all that, Jesus still lives today to help, heal, provide, and bless those He loves.

Here's a serious question and one that doesn't come up often in conversation. But take a minute to think about your life and how you view eternity. What have you heard before?

So, What If You Reject Christ? Where Will You Spend Eternity?

I can't candy-coat the truth. If you reject Christ and decide to live your life according to whatever rules you want to follow, here's what you can expect at the end of your life— spending all of eternity in hell.

Hell is described in the Bible as the most terrible place you'd ever want to be. It's a place where you are constantly pestered by creatures, and it's very hot. There's no water to drink, and you can't get any relief from this pit of hell. You can look up these scriptures in the Bible for yourself. But hell is a place of weeping (Matthew 8:12), wailing (Matthew 13:42), gnashing of teeth (Matthew 13:50), darkness (Matthew 25:30), flames (Luke 16:24), burning (Isaiah 33:14), and torments (Luke 16:23). If I was asked to describe hell in just two words, it would be *everlasting torment*!

Please see the next page to learn more about a relationship with God. If you enter by this gate, the narrow gate through Jesus, I can promise you you'll be in heaven after this life. God created you to have a relationship with Him. He loves you dearly! Please open your heart to learn about Jesus and how you can have a relationship with Him.

~ God Loves You ~
Learn about a Relationship with God

❖

Nobody can go back and start a new beginning.
But anyone can start today and make a new ending. [127]

If you've gone to church but have never heard about knowing God personally and having a personal relationship with Him through Christ, please take a comfortable seat and let me tell you about the best friend you could ever have!

God is a warm and caring heavenly Father who is always faithful and loving to His dear children. Before the sun, moon, and stars were ever created, God had a purpose for your life. He thought about you long ago, even before He fashioned the intricate details of your character, intellect, and personality. He also designed your physique and decided on the great talents you'd be able to share with the world.

But more than anything, God loves you. And that's precisely why He wants to have a relationship with you. It stands to reason too that if you love someone, you'll want to spend time with them; you'll want to nurture that relationship. And because God cares about us so much, He is often sad and hurt by the way we live. He never intended for us to be afraid, worried, depressed, angry, or impatient. Instead, God intended us to be joyful and fulfilled in a relationship with Him.

Because He is such a great and awesome God, when you put your trust completely in Him, your life will never be the same. Now, this doesn't mean you won't ever have a problem. But through the valleys and up to the breathtaking mountaintop moments of your life, He will be there to guide, protect, comfort, and strengthen you. And while we as human beings are limited by our own abilities, God has no limitations, and He does not change. Every challenge, concern, and everything else in between can be transformed by His power working in your life. There's nothing too difficult for God!

Today as you're reading this, all you need to do to have a relationship with God is say a little prayer. You simply need to invite God's Son, Jesus, to come into your heart.

Christ died on the cross for your sins—fear, worry, anger, impatience, pride, living for yourself—the things that keep you separated from a holy God. Religion, philosophy, and good works have always been humankind's attempt to reach God. Christ's death on the cross was God reaching down to humans to bring us back into a relationship with Him, the living God. But Jesus not only died for us; He rose again! And His victory over death means you can have victory in your life and know that you have eternal life as well!

~ God Loves You ~
Prayer to Know Christ as Your Savior

Dear Lord Jesus,

I know that I've done many things wrong throughout my life, and I ask for Your forgiveness. I believe You died on the cross for my sins (those things that keep me separated from a holy God). I also believe You rose from the dead, Jesus. Today I turn from my sins and ask You to come into my heart and life. I want to start trusting and following You as my Lord and Savior. Thank You for forgiving me and loving me. Thank You also for my new life in Christ as well as eternal life. Amen.

If you prayed that prayer,
on the next page, you'll be welcomed into the family of God.

~ God Loves You ~
Welcome to the Family of God

Living for God

As you live for God, you will experience victory by obeying God's Word, the Bible. To grow in your faith, make sure you find a church where Christ is preached—and start attending. There you will meet other believers who will help keep you encouraged in your faith.

If you prayed the above prayer, welcome to the family of God!

If You Asked Christ into Your Life

As the author of this book, I'd love to know if you prayed to receive Christ. Please take just a moment to email me at the book's email address, GodsPreciousGold2@gmail.com. To separate your response from spam, please title your message "I Received Christ." I promise to respond to you with some encouraging words. Again, welcome to the family of God!

Thank you so much!

Reference Section

Nanci's Blog—Meet the Author

What's a Blog?

A blog is an online web page. I update my blog periodically. In the blog, I share information about the book, book signings, and other helpful information.

Current Blog: Please visit my current blog at *nancigravill.wordpress.com.*

Meet the Author—Nanci J. Gravill

I have always loved words. That's because I've always recognized their ability to encourage, bring about change, and give hope.

With more than forty years of writing experience, I've used my creative gifts to teach language arts in three public school districts and at Cuyahoga Community College Western Campus, teaching seniors about writing. In the corporate sector, any employer that found out that I could write and loved it put me to work! I've written a variety of projects over the years, including technical reports, magazine articles, restaurant reviews for *Northern Ohio Live* magazine, newsletters, form letters, press releases, radio shows, fundraiser materials, sales literature, all sorts of promotional materials, poems, greeting card copy, song lyrics, and two books, *Fresh Hope ... Cleveland* (2012) and now my first devotional book, *More Precious Than Gold.*

I earned a bachelor of arts degree in promotional communications from Cleveland State University and three years toward another degree in individual and family development (Kent State University). You can read more about the book on my current blog at *nancigravill.wordpress.com.*

Endnotes

1 *Billy Graham's Answer: What Is Sin?,* Billy Graham Evangelical Association, accessed April 5, 2019, https://billygraham.org/story/billy-grahams-answer-what-is-sin-are-all-sins- equal-in-gods-eyes/.

2 "Dave Samples Quotes," Goodreads, accessed October 18, 2018, https://www.goodreads.com/author/quotes/14588934.Dave_Samples.

3 "Waiting on God Quotes," Goodreads, accessed October 18, 2018, https://www.goodreads.com/quotes/tag/waiting-on-god.

4 "Joyce Meyer Quotes," Goodreads, accessed October 18, 2018, https://www.goodreads.com/author/quotes/8352.Joyce_Meyer.

5 Joyce Meyer, *Power Thoughts Devotional,* (Nashville: Faith Words Publishing, 2013), 14.

6 "The GEICO Gecko orders Lemon Pie at the Diner," Geico, accessed February 10, 2019, https://www.google.com/search?q= geico+commercial+lemon+meringue+pie&client=.

7 *"Where Real Courage Comes From,"* Desiring God blog, accessed February 10, 2019, https://www.desiringgod.org/articles-where-real-courage-comes-from.

8 "Where Real Courage Comes From."

9 "Everyday Answers with Joyce Meyer," Joyce Meyer Ministries, accessed November 9, 2021, https://joycemeyer.org/everydayanswers/ea-teachings/how-to-boldly-move-forward-even-when-you-are-afraid.org.

10 "The Briefing Blog," Matthias Media, accessed December 11, 2018, http://thebriefing.com.au/2010/04/mental-toughness-and-the-living-god/.

11 "An FBI Agents 5 Steps to Developing Mental Toughness," Inc., https://www.inc.com/justin-bariso/an-fbi-agent-s-5-steps-to-developing-mental-toughness.html, accessed November 9, 2021.

12 "Mental Toughness," Wikipedia, accessed April 28, 2021, https://en.wikipedia.org/wiki/Mental_toughness.

13 "5 Characteristics of a Strong Mind," Michael Hyatt & Co, accessed November 10, 2021, https://michaelhyatt.com/strong-minded/.

14 "Mental Toughness and Following Christ," Church and Gospel blog, accessed January 10, 2019, https://www.churchandgospel.com/2017/04/12/mental-toughness-and-following-christ/.

15 "Pastor Andy Stanley Quotes," based on John 11: The Concept of Glory," Grace Church Singles Ministry, April 2011.

16 Joyce Meyer, *Change Your Words, Change Your Life: Understanding the Power of Every Word You Speak* (Nashville: FaithWords, October 2013), introduction.

17   "Change Your Words Quotes," Quotes.Pub, accessed November 10, 2021, https://quotes.pub/search?q=-Marguerite+Schumann.

18   Charles F. Stanley's *30 Life Principles: A Study for Growing in Knowledge and Understanding of God,* (Atlanta, Georgia: InTouch Ministries, 2008), 38.

19   Alvin VanderGriend, *Love to Pray: A 40-Day Devotional for Deeping Your Prayer Life* (Terre Haute: Harvest Prayer Ministries, 2004), 8–14.

20   "Prayer: The Billy Graham Library," Blog from the Billy Graham library, accessed November 10, 2021, https://billygrahamlibrary.org/5-quotes-on-prayer-from-billy-Graham/.

21   "Inspirational, Prayer, and Life Lesson Quotes," VeeroesQuotes, accessed April 2018, https://veeroesquotes.com/worry-prayer-quote/.

22   Sarah Young, *Jesus Calling: Enjoying Peace in His Presence* (Nashville: Thomas Nelson, 2004), 369.

23   "Germany Kent's Quotes on Blessings," All Christian Quotes, accessed February 14, 2020, https://www.allchristianquotes.org/quotes/Germany_Kent/8371/.

24   "English Dictionary," Lexico, assessed October 18, 2018, https://www.lexico.com/en/definition/gift.

25   Google Online Dictionary, Google, accessed October 18, 2018, https://www.google.com/search?q=-google+online+dictionary&client blessing%20in%20disguise.

26   "Google Online," Google, accessed March 10, 2020, https://google.com/search?q=google+online+dictionary &client lift.

27   "Charles Swindoll Encouragement Quotes," AZ Quotes, accessed March 10, 2020, https://www.azquotes.com/quote/867733.

28   *"What are psalms, hymns, and spiritual songs?"* Got Questions: Your Questions. Biblical Answers, accessed October 18, 2018,Gotquestions.org/psalms-hymns-spiritual- songs.ht*ml.*

29   *"Step Into the Encouragement* Zone," Turing Point Ministries, Oneplace.com, accessed October 18, 2018, https://www.crosswalk.com/faith/spiritual-life/inspiring-quotes/30-christian-quotes-about-thankfulness.html.

30   Charles F. Stanley, "Charles F. Stanley's 30 Life Principles: A Study for Growing in Knowledge and Understanding of God, (Atlanta, Georgia: InTouch Ministries, 2008), 33.

31   "Charles F. Stanley's 30 Life Principles," 43.

32   "Charles F. Stanley's 30 Life Principles," 127.

33   *"30 Beautiful Thankfulness Quotes to Bring Blessings of Joy and Gratitude,"* Crosswalk.com, accessed October 18, 2018, https://www.crosswalk.com/faith/spiritual-life/inspiring-quotes/30-christian-quotes-about-thankfulness.html.

34   "What about Happiness: 31 Benefits of Gratitude," Happier Human, accessed October 12, 2017, https://www.happierhuman.com/benefits-of-gratitude/.

35   Max Lucado, *You'll Get Through This: Hope and Help for Your Turbulent Times,* (Nashville: Thomas Nelson, 2015), 94–96.

36   Lucado, "You'll Get Through This."

37   Craig Groeschel, *#Struggles: Following Jesus in a Selfie-Centered World,* (Grand Rapids: Zondervan, October 2015), introduction.

38   Pastor James McDonald's comment on *Walking in the Word Ministry,* August 8, 2018.

39   Charles Grandison Finney Quotes, Goodreads, accessed January 25, 2019, https://www.goodreads.com/author/quotes/ 4645522.-Charles_Grandison_Finney.

40   "Anne Sexton Quotes," Goodreads, accessed May 3, 2019, https://www.goodreads.com/author/quotes/26814.Anne_Sexton.

41   "How to Encounter God through Journaling," Crosswalk.com, accessed August 8, 2008, http://www.crosswalk.com/faith/spiritual-life/how-to-encounter-god-through-journaling-11579830.html.

42   "3 Ways God Lightens Our Load," Jesus Calling blog, accessed November 12, 2021, https://www.jesuscalling.com/blog/3-ways-god-lightens-our-load/.

43   "3 Ways God Lightens Our Load."

44   David Rawlings, *The Baggage Handler*, (Nashville: Thomas Nelson, 2019), Amazon intro.

45   "10 Ways to Detox Your Soul Right Now," Crosswalk.com, accessed April 3, 2021, https://www.crosswalk.com/faith/spiritual-life/detoxify-your-soul.html.

46   "10 Ways to Detox Your Soul."

47   "Detox Your Soul: Four Spiritual Habits from the Psalms," Desiring God, accessed November 8, 2021, https://www.desiringgod.org/articles/detox-your-soul.

48   "Shakespeare Quotes," eNotes, assessed November 10, 2021, https://www.enotes.com/shakespeare-quotes/nothing-either-good-bad-but-thinking-makes.

49   "Your Life Is Shaped by Your Thoughts," Pastor Rick Warren, assessed January 4, 2020, https://pastorrick.com/devotional/english/your-life-is-shaped-by-your-thoughts4/.

50   "Dr Caroline Leaf – Bring Toxic Thoughts Into Captivity," YouTube, accessed November 15, 2021, https://www.youtube.com/watch?v=ZczIP_79jXs.

51   "Bring Toxic Thoughts Into Captivity."

52   Dr Caroline Leaf, *Switch On Your Brain: The Key to Peak Happiness, Thinking, and Health*, (Ada, Michigan: Baker Books, 2015), Publisher's Description.

53   "Switch On Your Brain."

54   "Joel Osteen Quotes," Brainy Quotes, accessed November 12, 2021, https://www.brainyquote.com/authors/joel-osteen-quotes.

55   "Joel Osteen Quotes on Blessings to Others," AZ Quotes, accessed November 12, 2021, https://www.azquotes.com/quote/578089.

56   "Operation Blessing promotional materials," received May 6, 2021, 2 Corinthians 9:6 ESV.

57   "Brian Houston Quotes," Goodreads, accessed November 11, 2021, https://www.goodreads.com/author/quotes/1097119.Brian_Houston.

58   "The Theology of Wholeness," FaithGateway, accessed May 5, 2019, https://www.faithgateway.com/theology-wholeness/#.YY23N7iyPAY.

59   "Mental Illness Statistics," National Institute of Mental Health, accessed May 15, 2019, https://www.nimh.nih.gov/health/statistics/mental-illness.

60   "What We Do," National Alliance on Mental Illness, accessed May 15, 2019, https://nami.org/About-NAMI/What-We-Do.

61   "Sean Covey Quotes," Goodreads, accessed February 17, 2018, https://www.goodreads.com/author/show/38343.Sean_Covey.

62   Dr. Henry Cloud, *The Law of Happiness: How Spiritual Wisdom and Modern Science Can Change Your Life*, (New York: First Howard Books, 2011), 16 -17.

63   Cloud, *The Law of Happiness*, 16 -17.

64   "Happy Habits: 12 Habits to Improve Overall Happiness in Life," The Wanderlust Worker, accessed August 12, 2017, https://www.wanderlustworker.com/the-happy-habits-12-habits-to-improve-your-over-all-happiness-in-life/.

65   "Happy Habits."

66   "Lord Byron Quotes," Brainy Quotes, assessed June 20, 2018, https://www.brainyquote.com/quotes/lord_byron_378386.

67   "Happy Habits."

68   "Denis Waitley Quotes," Brainy Quotes, accessed August 12, 2017, https://www.brainyquote.com/authors/denis-waitley-quotes.

69   "Inspirational Words of Wisdom," 73 Joy Quotes, accessed February 20, 2021, wow4u.com/joy/.

70   "Maintaining Joy," Crosswalk.com, accessed November 14, 2021, https://www.crosswalk.com/devo-tionals/in-touch/in-touch-jan-25-2010-11625291.html.

71   Kay Warren Quote heard at Ladies Latte, Grace Church, October 14, 2019.

72   "What is Joy?" Focus on the Family, assessed November 11, 2021, Focusonthefamily.com/parenting/what-is-joy.

73   "Psalm 32 – The Blessings of Forgiveness, Protection, and Guidance," Enduring Word, accessed November 14, 2021, https://enduringword.com/bible-commentary/psalm-32/.

74   "Are You Chasing Happiness or Holiness?," Desiring God, accessed August 7, 2017, https://www.desiringgod.org/articles/are-you-chasing-happiness-or-holiness.

75   "Webster's 1828 Dictionary: Holiness," King James Bible Dictionary, accessed August 7, 2017, http://kingjamesbibledictionary.com-/Dictionary/holiness.

76   "Following Jesus 101: Joy," Wanda Ball blog, accessed March 5, 2021, http://wanda-ball.com/blog/transcribe-the-word-unspeakable-joy-bible-study/.

77   "J. I. Packer Quotes," Goodreads, accessed October 25, 2018, https://www.goodreads.com/quotes/1151789-wisdom-is-the-power-to-see-and-the-inclination-to.

78   "Why Solomon Asked for Wisdom," Immanuel Bible Church blog, accessed July 6, 2021, http://www.discoverjoy.com/blog/2016/4/11/why-solomon-asked-for-wisdom.

79   "Joyce Meyer Quote," Enjoying Everyday Life TV Show, heard September 14, 2017.

80   "C. Neil Strait Quote," PassItOn, accessed May 20, 2018, https://www.passiton.com/inspiration-al-quotes/7669-kindness-is-anything-that-lifts-another-person.

81   "Leprosy." Wikipedia, accessed May 20, 2018, https://en.wikipedia.org/wiki/Leprosy.

82   "20 Good Quotes about Attitude," What Christians Want to Know, accessed April 20, 2019, https://www.whatchristianswanttoknow.com/20-good-christian-quotes-about-attitude/.

83   "The Attitude Jesus Wants from All of His Followers, And How to Get It," Relevant, accessed May 3, 2017, https://www.relevantmagazine.com/faith/the-attitude-jesus-wants-from-all-of-his-followers/.

84   "Attitude Jesus Wants from His Followers."

85   "Attitude Jesus Wants from His Followers."

86   "Charles Swindoll Attitude Quote," Kutztown University, accessed May 2, 2019, faculty.kutztown.edu/friehauf/attitude.html.

87   "Women of the Word: How to Study the Bible with Both Our Hearts and Our Minds," Goodreads, accessed August 10, 2021, https://www.goodreads.com/book/show/19353107-women-of-the-word.

88   "131 Woodrow Kroll Quotes," Christian Quotes, accessed April 2, 2019, https://www.christianquotes.info/quotes-by-author/woodrow-kroll-quotes/.

89   Nik Wallenda, *Facing Fear: Step Out in Faith and Rise Above What's Holding You Back (Nashville: Thomas Nelson, 2020),* Amazon book description.

90   *"Facing Fear."*

91   Max Lucado, *Imagine Your Life Without Fear* (Nashville: Thomas Nelson, 2009), Amazon introduction.

92   "When You Mess Up, Do you Run to God or Run from Him?", Women Living Well Ministries, accessed March 1, 2021, https://womenlivingwell.org/2016/05/when-you-mess-up-do-you-run-from-god-or-run-to-him/.

93   W.B. Freeman Concepts, Inc., *God's Little Devotional Book on Success*, (Tulsa, Oklahoma, Honor Books), 54.

94   Nola Ochs, Wikipedia, accessed April 10, 2019, https://en.wikipedia.org/wiki/Nola_Ochs.

95   "Nola Ochs."

96   *"Three Ways to Improve Your Memory with New Learning,"* Amen Clinics, accessed November 12, 2021, https://www.amenclinics.com/blog/ways-to-improve-your-memory-with-new-learning/.

97   "How Do I Grow As A Christian?, "thinke {think eternity}blog," accessed June 15, 2019, https://thinke.org/blog/how-to-grow-as-christian.

98   "Love Is More Than A Feeling: The Green Bean Club," nancigravill.wordpress.com, https://nancigravill.wordpress.com/2013/12/21/love-is-more-than-just-a-feeling-the-green-bean-club/.

99   "Dr. Myles Munroe Quotes," Goodreads, accessed June 2018, https://www.goodreads.com/quotes/1252289-be-fruitful-god-s-command-in-genesis-1-28-is-most-often.

100   Candy Christmas guest on The Huckabee Show, TBN, December 24, 2017.

101   "Candy Christmas."

102   *"Homelessness In Nashville Spikes 10 Percent,"* Tennessean, accessed November 12, 2021, https://www.tennessean.com/story/news/2016/12/14/homelessness-nashville-spikes-10-percent/95419066/.

103   "Candy Christmas," Cross Rhythms, accessed October 18, 2019, https://www.crossrhythms.co.uk/articles/music/Candy_Christmas_A_Southern_gospel_star_finds_purpose_helping_the_homeless/41281/p1/.

104   Candy Christmas, *On The Other Side: Life Changing Stories From Under the Bridge*, (Abilene, Texas: Leafwood Publishers, 2010), Amazon introduction.

105   "Alistair Begg Quotes," Goodreads, accessed June 15, 2019, https://www.goodreads.com/author/quotes/387751.Alistair_Begg.

106   "72 Forgiveness Quotes," Inspirational Words of Wisdom, assessed June 15, 2019, https://www.wow4u.com/qforgiveness/ .

107   *"Anger, Injustice, Unforgiveness, and Cancer,"* Sue Hannibal Intuitive Behaviorist, accessed May 2, 2020, https://suehannibal.com/blog/anger-injustice-unforgiveness-and-cancer/.

108   "D.L. Moody Quotes," A Z Quotes, accessed November 14, 2021, https://www.azquotes.com/quote/523168.

109   Ruth Graham guest on The Huckabee" show TBN Network, May 2, 2020.

110   Pat Robertson on Christian Broadcasting Network, CBN's "700 Club" talk show, April 30, 2020.

111   "76 Quotes About Forgiveness," Christian Quotes, accessed May 2, 2020, https://www.christianquotes.info/quotes-by-topic/quotes-about-forgiveness/.

112   Emily Dickinson, " 'Hope' is the thing with feathers" in *Final Harvest: Emily Dickinson's Poems*, Thomas H. Johnson, ed. Boston: Little, Brown & Company, 1961, 34.

113   "Corrie ten Boom," Wikipedia, accessed April 13, 2020, https://en.wikipedia.org/wiki/Corrie_ten_Boom.

114   "Why the Anchor? And What Is a Chrismon?," Reasons for Hope *Jesus, https://reasonsforhopejesus.com/chrismon-anchor/. accessed October 3, 2018).

115   "RC Sproul's 'hope' quote," Quotefancy, accessed April 17, 2020, https://quotefancy.com/quote/1490351/R-C-Sproul-Hope-is-called-the-anchor-of-the-soul-because-it-gives-stability-to-the.

116   "Anchor," King James Bible Dictionary, accessed November 14, 2021, http://www.kingjamesbibledictionary.com/Dictionary/anchor.

117   Joel Osteen heard at Lakewood Church, on TBN February 10, 2019.

118   "This Is The Most Common of the 5 Love Languages," HuffPost, accessed November 14, 2021, https://www.huffpost.com/entry/most-common-love-language_n_5b4f906be4b0b15aba8b1d2c.

119   "Love," Wikipedia, accessed May 2018, https://en.wikipedia.org/wiki/Love.

120   "Love."

121   "The Shape of True Love," Proverbs 31 Ministries, accessed November 14, 2021, https://proverbs31.org/read/devotions/full-post/2015/02/13/the- shape-of-true-love.

122   C. S. Lewis, *Letters to an American Lady,* (Grand Rapids, Michigan: W.B. Eerdmans Publishing Co., 1967), Volume 3.

123   "Every Ending Is Always a New Beginning," Love Revolution, accessed November 15, 2021, https://loverevolutionblog.com/every-ending-is-always-a-new-beginning/.

124   "The Meanest Man in Texas", Sermon Central, accessed July 12, 2019, http://sermoncentral.com/sermon-illustrations/sermon-illustrations-about-the-meanest-man-in-Texas.

125   "Woodrow Kroll Quote," Christian Quotes, accessed May 4, 2020, https://www.christianquotes.info/quotes-by-author/woodrow-kroll-quotes/.

126   "50 Christian Quotes to Inspire Your Faith Every Day," Crosswalk, accessed May 10, 2020, https://www.crosswalk.com/faith/spiritual-life/inspiring-quotes/30-inspiring-christian-quotes.html.

127   Maria Robinson Quotes, Goodreads, accessed October 5, 2019, https://www.goodreads.com/author/quotes/444986.Maria_Robinson.

Printed in the United States
by Baker & Taylor Publisher Services